Fourteen Plays for the Church

ROBERT SCHENKKAN

AND

KAI JURGENSEN (ed.)

Fourteen Plays

FOR THE CHURCH

"I have heard of Thee by the hearing of
the ear: but now mine eye seeth Thee."
Job. *xlii,* 5

New Brunswick

RUTGERS UNIVERSITY PRESS

1948

Bible, plays

For Jean and Peggy

PREFACE

THE CHURCH today is turning more and more to the use of drama as an educational and inspirational medium through which to reach the congregation. In response to this growing demand there has been an ever greater flow of fine modern dramas designed for production on church stages.

There is, however, a great heritage of magnificent, traditional church drama which has necessarily been ignored to a great extent because it is available only in foreign or archaic languages, and has never been arranged for production in the modern church. It is this gap which the present volume is intended to fill, at least in part.

All but one of the plays included here are representative of a considerable body of drama developed during the middle ages for the purpose of instruction in matters of faith. They have the qualities of naïveté and simplicity which lend them a charm and interest unequalled by more sophisticated drama. At the same time their authors were, in many cases, craftsmen and poets of uncommon skill. The editors have attempted to recapture these qualities of the originals while making the language understandable to the modern actor and audience.

One of the chief appeals of these plays is that some may be done in the church proper, since many of them were originally designed for that purpose and served as illustrations to the special services for Christmas, Easter, and other holidays. The majority of modern religious dramas cannot be so produced. Yet what more inspiring or proper setting can be found than the church itself? And what could be a more fitting time for the performance of plays which are in themselves an act of worship than in conjunction with the service itself?

Naturally, the greater portion of these traditional plays belongs to the Christmas and Easter seasons, and the present volume consists in large part of material for these two occasions. But there are others which fall in neither category, yet provide moving drama and memorable religious experience. Such an awesome and magnificent expression of faith as *The Book of Job*, such a tender expression of devotion as *The Sacrifice of Isaac*, should no longer be left to the library and the occasional text, but should serve again the inspirational dramatic purpose for which they were designed.

A few of these plays include scenes of secular comedy not entirely appropriate for the church proper. They were, in fact, produced outside the church by medieval trade guilds. Although the purpose and import of these, too, is predominantly religious, the editors suggest that they be presented in the recreation room, or some other suitable place adjoining the church. The remainder of the plays has been arranged for production in transept and chancel.

It is our hope that this volume will be of assistance to the many directors of church drama who must carry on the unceasing search for new material which has the dignity and the reverence befitting its purpose and locale.

The editors wish to express their deep gratitude to the following gentlemen. Had it not been for their knowledge and patient aid and advice, this book might never have been written: Rev. David Yates, Chapel Hill, North Carolina; Professor George R. Coffman and Professor Robert Sharpe, Department of English; Professor Urban T. Holmes, De-

partment of Romance Languages; Professor Lynn Gault,
Department of Dramatic Art; Francis Bliss, Department of
Classics; and Wilton Mason, Department of Music, all of the
University of North Carolina.

Kai Jurgensen
Robert Schenkkan

Chapel Hill, North Carolina
March 1948

CONTENTS

Plays for the Christmas Season

Plays for the Easter Season

Plays for Other Occasions

Notes on Production

PLAYS FOR
The Christmas Season

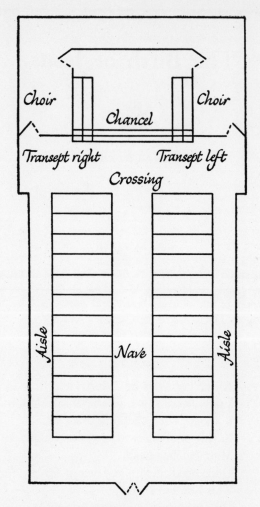

TYPICAL CHURCH FLOOR PLAN

The Birth of Jesus

CHARACTERS:

Mary
Joseph
The Choir

THE SCENE:

The scene is Bethlehem. A cattle shed with a manger.
The place representing the shed is placed in the
chancel of the church. MARY and JOSEPH are by the
manger. The CHOIR is in the choir-stalls.

[*Playing time*: *10 minutes*]

JOSEPH

All ruling God in Trinity!
I pray You, Lord, in all Your might,
Look to Your simple servant here
In this poor place where she tonight
Must lay her head.
God, make it safe and warm for us,
This humble shed.

For we have hunted everywhere
Through all of Bethlehem today.
So many people are in town,

We cannot find a place to stay.
The crowd has so increased,
There's nowhere else for us to sleep,
But with the beasts.

And if we stay here all night long,
We shall be open to the weather.
The walls are down on every side,
The roof is ruined altogether.
The wind blows through.
Speak, Mary, wife, what's your advice?
What shall we do?

For now we really are in need.
As you can see, we are forlorn;
For here is neither bed nor bedding,
And we are tired out and worn,
And need to rest.
Now Gracious God, in all Your mercy,
Heed our request!

MARY

Ah, Joseph, lift your spirits up.
God will show us, as you know,
For in this place He will be born,
Who will save us from our woe.
So do not mourn,
For, sir, you know the time is near
When he'll be born.

JOSEPH

It's better, then, for us to stay
Here in this humble place tonight.

MARY

Yes, Joseph, it's His will, I'm sure.

JOSEPH

Why, then I wish we had some light,
If need should be.
The night is getting darker now,
It seems to me.

I'll go at once and get a light,
And find some fuel to bring back, too.

MARY

Then Joseph, husband, go with God
Who governs everything we do
Through His great might.
And may I have His blessing, too,
In this, my plight.

(JOSEPH *leaves through the door of the transept.*)

Oh, I am joyful in my heart,
I am all clad in comfort clear!
Now from my body will be born
Both God and man, united here.
Blest may He be!

(*The lights on the manger go out. There is a brief
musical interlude. At its close the lights come up again
on* MARY *with the child in her arms.*)

Jesus, my Son, who is so dear,
Is born to me.

(*She worships the* CHILD.)

Hail, my Lord God! Hail, Prince of Peace!

Hail, my Father! And hail, my Son!
Hail, Leader in the war on sin!
Hail, God and Man, alive in One!
Hail, through Whose might
The whole great world did first begin,
Darkness and light!

O, Son, in my humility,
Allow, sweet Son, I beg of You,
That I may hold You on my knee
And clothe You in this simple dress.
Grant me Your bliss!
As I'm Your mother, chosen to be
In steadfastness.

JOSEPH
(*Enters the transept.*)

Ah, Lord, the weather is so cold!
The coldest night I ever knew!
I beg God help those who are old,
And even more the ones who're ill.
This prayer I pray.
And in Your grace myself enfold,
As best You may.
(*The star blazes above.*)

Ah, Lord, my God, what light is this
That shines so suddenly and clear?
I couldn't say, for my soul's bliss.
When I see Mary—and I am near—
I'll question her.
(*He advances toward the shed.*)

The Birth of Jesus

Ah, thanks to God, for I am here.
(*He enters the shed.*)

MARY

You're welcome, sir.

JOSEPH

Well, Mary, tell me how you feel.

MARY

All our woe is gone away!

JOSEPH

Ah, Mary, what sweet thing is that?

MARY

It is my Son, the truth to say,
My holy Son.

JOSEPH

How glad I am to see the day
This Child has come.

I marvel greatly at the light
That shines so brightly in this space.
It is, indeed, a wondrous thing!

MARY

He has ordained it by His grace,
That a star adorn
The heavens high above the place
Where He is born.

For Balaam told it long ago,
A shining star would rise on high;
And of a maiden should be born
A Son who would men purify
From bitter care.
And, sure, it was my Son and I
He spoke of there.

JOSEPH

Now, welcome, fairest boy of all!
I'll honor you with main and might!
Hail, my Maker! Hail, Christ Jesus!
Hail, Royal King, the Root of Right!
Hail, Savior Son!
Hail, my Lord, Giver of Light!
Hail, blessed One!

MARY

O Lord, of Whom the prophets said
That You will conquer all the world.
As You can see, here is no bed,
And so, dear Son, I beg of You,
Though it be mean,
Accept this humble crib instead,
Two beasts between.

And I shall wrap you up, my child,
With such poor clothes as we have here.

JOSEPH

O, Mary, see the beasts, so mild,
They act so loving and so dear

Before His grace.
It seems as if they are beguiled
By His sweet face.

MARY

They know their Lord, I'm sure they do.
They worship Him with all their might.
The night is cold, and bitter, too;
They try as hard the cold to fight
As their poor means afford.
That's why they let their breath alight
Upon their Lord.

My Son's asleep now. Blessings on Him!
Lying warm and smiling so.

JOSEPH

Now it's fulfilled, I see it plain,
What Abakuk said so long ago,
Wisest of all priests:
He said our Savior we would know,
Asleep between two beasts.

And now we see the very sight.

MARY

O, yes, it's true. He is the One.

JOSEPH

Honor and worship, both day and night,
Be given You, my Lord and Son,
As is in every way Your right!

And, Lord, I pledge myself to You
With all my might.

MARY

Oh, merciful and mighty King,
My God, my Lord, my Son so free,
I serve Thy will in everything,
And I, too, pledge myself to Thee,
Heart, hand, and head.
I beg Your blessing on us three,
In holy dread!

(*The* CHOIR *forms a living curtain in front of the
manger and sings a Christmas hymn of praise while*
JOSEPH *and* MARY *exit behind them.*)

Herod and the Kings

CHARACTERS:

Mary	*Two Women*
Herod	*First King*
Herod's Son	*Second King*
A Soldier	*Third King*
The Angel	*Scribe*
The Shepherds	*The Choir*

THE SCENE:

Three places are represented. The cattle shed is set in the chancel; MARY is seated by the manger. HEROD is seated, perhaps on a platform, in the transept right, which represents his throne room. With him are his SON and a SOLDIER, both standing. The SHEPHERDS are standing in the transept left, which represents their field. The CHOIR is in the choir stalls.

[*Playing time: 12 minutes*]

THE ANGEL

(*Entering the transept doors, left. The* SHEPHERDS *fall to their knees as they see him.*)

Fear not; for behold, I bring you tidings of great joy, which shall be to all people; for unto you there is born this day in the city of David, a Savior of the world. And this shall be a sign unto you: You shall find the Babe wrapped in swaddling clothes and lying in a manger between two beasts.

CHOIR

(*Singing.*)

Glory to God in the Highest, and on earth peace, good will to men! Alleluia! Alleluia!

(*The* ANGEL *goes out as he came in.*)

THE SHEPHERDS

(*Rising to their feet, speaking in unison.*)

Let us now go to Bethlehem and see this thing which is come to pass, which the Lord has done and made known to us.

(*As they reach the* CHOIR, TWO WOMEN *in the fore-front speak.*)

THE WOMEN

(*In unison.*)

Whom seek you in the manger, O shepherds? Tell us.

THE SHEPHERDS

The Savior, the Christ, the Infant Lord, wrapped in swaddling clothes, according to the words of the Angel.

THE WOMEN

(*Pointing.*)

The little One is here with Mary, His mother, of whom, long ago, Isaiah prophesied: "Behold, a virgin shall conceive and bear a son."

THE SHEPHERDS

(Enter the chancel, and, falling on their knees, worship the Child.)

Hail, King of the ages!

(They turn to the congregation.)

Come! Come! Come! Let us worship Him, for He alone is our Savior!

(Meanwhile, the KINGS *enter separately at the rear of the nave.)*

FIRST KING

(As he enters.)

This star is blazing very brightly!

SECOND KING

(Following.)

Its coming was foretold by the prophets, long ago.

FIRST KING

(To the THIRD KING *as he enters.)*

Peace to you, brother!

THIRD KING

Peace to you, also!

SECOND KING

And peace to you.

FIRST KING
(Pointing.)

Behold the star.

SECOND AND THIRD KINGS

Yes, behold the star.

FIRST KING

Let us go, then, and seek Him.
                    (*They proceed up the nave.*)

SECOND KING

And offer Him our gifts.

THIRD KING

I bring gold.

FIRST KING

I bring frankincense.

SECOND KING

And I bring myrrh.

THIRD KING

For all of us know that which is written: All
Kings shall worship Him, all nations serve Him.
          (*They arrive at the crossing and ask of the* CHOIR.)

SECOND KING

Where is He Who is born King of the Jews?

THIRD KING

Where is He Whose star has led us here to worship?
          (HEROD, *having seen them as they approached the
          crossing, has pantomimed alarm and interest. He sends
          a* SOLDIER *who intercepts them at the close of the pre-*

ceding speech before the CHOIR *can answer. He speaks:*)

SOLDIER

Of what nation are you? Where is your home?

FIRST KING

We are Chaldeans.

SOLDIER

Do you bring peace or war?

SECOND KING

We bring peace.

SOLDIER

What strange things bring you on these roads which you do not know? Where are you going?

THIRD KING

We are seeking the King of Kings, Whose birth is shown by this brightest of stars.

FIRST KING

Star-led, in search of the heralded King, furnished with gifts, we come to worship Him.

(*The* SOLDIER *returns to* HEROD *and kneels before him. Meanwhile, the* KINGS *pantomime conversation among themselves.*)

SOLDIER

Live, O King, forever!

HEROD

We welcome you.

SOLDIER

Lord, these three unknown men come from the East in search of a certain new-born King.

HEROD

Tell them to come here to me. I, myself want to ask them who they are and why they come.

SOLDIER

I shall do as you command, renowned King.
(*He goes to the* KINGS.)
King Herod summons you to his presence. Come quickly.
(*He leads the* KINGS *to* HEROD.)
Behold, my lord, the Kings!

HEROD
(*To the* KINGS.)

Who are you? Where do you come from? And why do you come here? Speak?

FIRST KING

We come because of a King.

SECOND KING

We are, ourselves, Kings—from Arabia.

THIRD KING

Yes, we have come to seek a King above Kings, to a maiden newly born.

HEROD

How do you know that He is born?

FIRST KING

We saw His star in the east.

HEROD

Do you believe that He reigns? Tell us.

SECOND KING

We do.

THIRD KING

And we have come with mystic gifts from a far country to worship Him. We will pay homage to the Triune God with three gifts.

(*The* KINGS *display their gifts.*)

FIRST KING

Gold, to symbolize a King.

SECOND KING

Frankincense, a God.

THIRD KING

And myrrh, a mortal.

HEROD

(*To the* SOLDIER)

You, soldier—order a scribe, learned in the law, to tell us what he finds in the Prophets concerning these things.

(*The* KINGS *and* HEROD *pantomime conversation.*)

SOLDIER

(*Goes to the nearer transept door and fetches the* SCRIBE *with his great book.*)

You are summoned before the King. Come quickly with the book of the prophets.

HEROD
(*To the* SCRIBE.)

O scribe, tell me if you see anything concerning this boy written in the book!

SCRIBE

(*Turning the leaves of the book until he seems to find the prophecy.*)

I see, my lord, in the lines of the prophets, that the Christ is born in Bethlehem of Judea, in the city of David. The prophet has foretold it.

(*He hands the book to* HEROD *who is incredulous. When* HEROD *has read the prophecy, he hurls the book angrily to the floor, but his* SON *advances to him, attempting to calm him.*)

HEROD'S SON

All hail, renowned father!
All hail, illustrious king,
Who rules this mighty realm
And bears the royal sceptre!

HEROD

Oh, most beloved son,
Deserving of all praise,
And bearing in your name
The pomp of regal glory.

A King is born among us
Who is stronger yet than we.
I fear that He may force us
From our royal throne.

HEROD'S SON
(*Contemptuously*.)

Against this petty King,
Against this new-born Babe,
Command your son, O father,
To wage a mortal war.
> (HEROD *nods, pleased, then gestures the* KINGS, *who have been standing aside, to step before him again. They do so.*)

HEROD

Go then, and seek this Boy; and when you have found Him,
bring me word so that I, too, may come and worship Him.
> (*The* KINGS *turn and advance to the crossing, following the star, which they point out to one another.* HEROD *has not yet seen the star, but now, observing the gestures of the* KINGS, *both he and his* SON *discover it, and brandish their swords in anger.*)

FIRST KING

Look! The star we saw in the East leads us on again!

SECOND KING

How brightly it shines!
> (*At the crossing, the* KINGS *meet the* SHEPHERDS, *who are leaving the chancel and singing a Christmas hymn.*)

THIRD KING

Whom have you seen?

FIRST SHEPHERD

Just as the Angel told us, we found the Babe, wrapped in swaddling clothes, and lying in a manger between two beasts.

(*The* SHEPHERDS *leave by the left transept door, and the* THREE KINGS *stand at the crossing, singing:*)

THE KINGS *

Heaven and earth and the wide, wide deep
Could never contain Him for all of their size.
He is born to us from out of the skies,
And lies in a manger asleep.
As the prophets foretold, it has come to pass,
He lies in the straw with the ox and the ass.
But the star rises bright,
His vigil to keep,
It shines and it blinds our eyes with its light.

(*They turn back towards the chancel.*)

FIRST WOMAN
(*In the* CHOIR.)

Who are these strangers that come bearing gifts?

FIRST KING

We are the Kings of Tharsis, of Arabia, and of Saba.

SECOND KING

We come bearing gifts to the new-born Christ, the King.

* For music to *The Song of the Kings*, see pp. 269 and 270.

THIRD KING

To the Lord, Whom we, led by a star, have come to worship.

SECOND WOMAN
(*Pointing to the manger.*)

Here is the Boy you seek. Now hasten to adore Him, for He is the Redeemer of the world.
(*They approach the manger.*)

FIRST KING

Hail, King of the Ages!

SECOND KING

Hail, God of Gods!

THIRD KING

Hail, Salvation of the dead!

FIRST KING
(*Kneeling.*)

I offer gold, the sign of kings.

SECOND KING
(*Kneeling.*)

I offer myrrh, the sign of Your mortality.

THIRD KING
(*Kneeling.*)

And I, frankincense, You very God!
(*They turn to leave and are met by the* ANGEL *who comes from the transept, left.*)

ANGEL

Now all which was written by the prophets is fulfilled.
When you return, avoid King Herod, and save the Child
from a cruel death.

(*He enters the chancel and stands by the manger.*)

FIRST KING

Praise be to God that He has warned us by His angel!

SECOND KING

Let us take another road so Herod will learn nothing
from us.

THIRD KING

And praise be to God, the Boy will be safe!

THE KINGS

(*Turn to the left, unseen by* HEROD; *exclaim together:*)

Oh, night of wonder!
We have seen the Lord!

FIRST KING

(*Addressing the* CHOIR.)

Rejoice, brothers!

SECOND KING

(*Fervently.*)

God is made man!

THIRD KING

(*Triumphantly.*)

Christ is born!

(The CHOIR *forms a living curtain before the manger and sings a triumphant hymn. The* KINGS *go out left;* HEROD *and his court, right.* MARY *and the* ANGEL *leave by the chancel door, behind the* CHOIR *curtain.)*

The Annunciation, the Birth, and the Shepherds

CHARACTERS:

Mary	*First Shepherd*
Joseph	*Second Shepherd*
Gabriel	*Third Shepherd*
An Angel	*The Choir*

THE SCENE:

Three places are represented. At transept right is the home of MARY and JOSEPH: MARY is seated alone. In the chancel, the cattle shed and manger of Bethlehem, empty. That portion of the nave which extends from the main door of the church halfway to the crossing will represent the fields of the SHEP-HERDS. It is empty. The CHOIR is in the choir stalls.

[*Playing time: 15 minutes.*]

GABRIEL

(*Enters the right transept door, appearing to* MARY, *who is seated there.*)

Hail, Mary, full of grace!
The Lord, our God, speaks forth through me.
Above all other women,
Lady, blessed may you be!

MARY

(*Frightened.*)

Almighty Father, keep me safe,
Beneath Your watchful eye,
For I am sorely troubled now,
Amazed, and know not why.

GABRIEL

O maiden, fear me not,
For I am sent from Heaven,
Herald of that King of Bliss;
His blessing you are given.

I salute your pure, sweet face,
Above all others, full of worth,
For you shall bloom with grace,
You shall conceive and bring to birth
God's own Son to live on earth.

MARY

But how is such a thing to be?

GABRIEL

The Holy Ghost shall sanctify
And brighten you with virtue
From Him Who is on high.

This Child that you shall bear
Is Second of the Trinity.
He shall offer man salvation
By grace of His Divinity.

MARY

Since it is the Good Lord's will
His Son on earth through me be sent,
As His handmaid I will submit,
And carry out my Lord's intent.

GABRIEL

I bless the day when you were born.
Now God in Trinity is conceived.
And so, farewell, Sweet Lady;
Your place in Heaven is achieved.
(*Music.* GABRIEL *leaves as he entered.* JOSEPH *comes into the transept, left, and crosses to* MARY.)

JOSEPH
(*Approaching her.*)

Bless you, Mary, dearest wife,
What are your tidings of good cheer?

MARY

I wait upon the good Lord's will,
My husband, Joseph dear.

JOSEPH
(*Looks at her searchingly.*)

Has anyone been here at all,
Since I have been away from you?

MARY

No man has been here, nor his like,
But God's own Messenger, and true.

JOSEPH

The words you speak are blasphemy!
It's plain to see you're great with child!
Tell me, woman, whose it is?

MARY

It's yours alone, my husband mild —

As you shall see yourself one day.

JOSEPH

Alas, how can you say, my own?

MARY

Believe me, husband.

JOSEPH

Husband? Yes, in name alone!

(*Turning away, he speaks as if to himself.*)
Ah, Joseph, go; you poor, old man;
You stand here like a helpless fool.
(*Turning back.*)
Ah, Mary, you have sinned against me;
To teach me in this painful school,

As much as I have cherished you!
(*Away.*)
Just see how I have been beguiled
All you old men who witness this,
And never wed so young a child.

(*To* MARY.)

Farewell! I leave you here alone.
You and your works may stay and moan.

(JOSEPH *leaves* MARY, *his head bowed.*)

I will no longer be deceived
By friend or foe.

(*In a sudden access of weariness and grief, he stops at the crossing.*)

I cannot go another step.
Oh, I am full of woe!

(*He lies down on the chancel steps as if to sleep. An* ANGEL *enters to him from the chancel door.*)

ANGEL
(*Standing above him.*)

Joseph, arise! Go home again!
Go home and see you comfort her,
Your Mary, who is free of stain;
For she has never wronged you, sir.

She has conceived, to her great fame,
God's Son, although she is a maid.
And He shall always bear the name
Of Jesus, Savior of the world.
Be not afraid.

(*The* ANGEL *leaves as he came.*)

JOSEPH
(*Rising.*)

These are truly joyful tidings,
That you, God's Messenger, impart.

I must go home at once to Mary!
                    (*He stops.*)
I thank You, Lord, with all my heart.

                    (*He hurries to* MARY.)
Ah, Mary, see! I kneel to you!
Forgive me for my words of hate.
Mercy, Mary! Now I know
The truth of your pure, holy state.

Although I disbelieved at first,
Mercy, Mary! While I may,
I'll never grieve you any more,
In earnest or in play.

MARY

The Lord above forgive you, Joseph,
As I forgive you, in His name.

JOSEPH

Thanks, gentle Mary, for your prayer.
But I must go to Bethlehem
And carry out my duty there.
Still, I am afraid to go away;
You shouldn't be alone this day.

MARY

No, Joseph, have no fear of that,
For I will keep you company
I trust in our Almighty God
To guard us everlastingly.

JOSEPH

I thank you, Mary, for your goodness,
And will, as on our way we plod.
Since we must go to Bethlehem,
Let's go together, then, with God.

(*They leave through the transept doors, right, behind them. The* CHOIR *sings a hymn of Advent. As
they finish,* JOSEPH *and* MARY *enter the transept left,
as if weary from their journey.*)

JOSEPH
(*As they approach the crossing.*)

We're now three leagues from Bethlehem.
And it is near the end of day,
You look so weary, Mary dear,
I wish you had some place to stay.

MARY

God have mercy on us, Joseph.
The time the prophets have foretold,
That time my Child, the King of Bliss,
Is to be born, will soon unfold.

Please, Joseph, lead me to some place,
Where I may rest in my distress.
Oh, Father, shed Your light on us,
And offer us Your blessedness.

JOSEPH
(*Leading her to the shed in the chancel.*)

My blessed Mary, you stay here
Within this shed, and I will go

To see if I can find some help.
This is the best advice I know.

MARY

I pray you, Joseph, go along.

JOSEPH
(*Going.*)

God be with you, I won't tarry.
(*He enters the transept right. Speaks again, to him-
self.*)
Now I'll go straight to Bethlehem
And get some help for my sweet Mary.

God grant her labor can be eased.
So my sweet Mary may be pleased.
(JOSEPH *goes out the right transept doors.*)

FIRST SHEPHERD
(*Appears at the rear of the nave and advances halfway
to the crossing, as if seeking, then turns.*)

O Lord, I cannot sleep;
Look down and save my friends and me.
They're lost, as are my sheep.
Brrr, it is so cold tonight.
It's nearly midnight now, I'm sure.
The weather's dark, so dim the light,
There's not a thing that you can see
Across this lonely moor.

I know. I'll roar it out.
What ho, my friends! How do you fare?
(*Two other* SHEPHERDS *appear at the rear of the nave.*)

SECOND SHEPHERD

Sim, I hear our brother shout,
He calls us from the hill.
It is his voice—if I hear right.
                    (FIRST SHEPHERD *keeps calling.*)
Let's go up! *Brrr,* it's chill!
Look, Sim, look! He's coming there!
I'm glad at last he is in sight.

                    (*They meet.*)
Brother, how did you get lost
And on such a bitter night?

FIRST SHEPHERD

Friends, there was a windy gust,
Blowing mist along with it.
That's what made me lose my way.
It nearly drove me to a fit.
Didn't know which way was right,
So I decided here I'd stay.

THIRD SHEPHERD

Brother, now the fear is gone.
It is very late at night.
Dawn will break upon us soon.
It is nearly day.
Let's sit down a spell and rest.
Eat and drink while yet we may.
Let's wait here until it's light.
That, I think, would be the best.

    (*The* SHEPHERDS *bring out their food, and are about
    to sit, when they behold the star.*)

Brothers, raise your eyes and look!
What's that shining out so bright?
Long as I have watched my flock,
No star like this has ever shone.
The time has come that was foretold:
Born of the purest maiden known,
On a freezing winter night,
A little Babe would bring us light,
Fulfilling all the prophecies of old.

FIRST SHEPHERD

Beyond a doubt your words are right!
It is as the prophets say:
A maid would bear a child as pure as light,
On the shortest winter day,
Near the middle of the night.

SECOND SHEPHERD

Blessed be the Trinity;
We will see that wondrous sight.
Let us kneel and pray, all three.

Since it is His holy will,
Though we are of humble worth,
That we understand it still,
Let us praise His awesome might,
While we live on earth.

> (The CHOIR *sings a verse of*: Glory to God in the
> Highest, *continues as the* SHEPHERDS *speak*.)

THIRD SHEPHERD

Hark! The Angels sing above!
Listen to the joyful sound!

FIRST SHEPHERD

These are tidings of great love,
That flood the world around.

"God's own Son to us is born,"
Says the star this winter morn.
(*The* CHOIR *ceases singing.*)

SECOND SHEPHERD

"Glory, glory to God in the highest,"
Was the song the Angels sang.
Weren't those the words that rang?

FIRST SHEPHERD

True enough. Now let's depart
And worship Him, with all our heart!
(*The* SHEPHERDS *sing as they come slowly down the nave.*)

(*Song*)*

As I rode out this past midnight,
Of three jolly shepherds I caught a sight;
And all about their fold a star shone bright.
They sang terli, terlow.
So merrily the shepherds their pipes can blow.
(*The* CHOIR *begins again*, Glory to God in the Highest. *The* SHEPHERDS *stop to listen.*)

JOSEPH
(*Entering the transept, right.*)

O Lord, this song I hear,
So solemn, pure and free,

* For music to *Terli Terlow*, see pp. 271 and 272.

Has swept away my fear.
My heart is filled with strange, sweet joy.
(*He comes in to* MARY.)

MARY

Ah, Joseph, husband, come to me.
My Child is born, the Holy Boy.

JOSEPH

Now welcome to me, Maker of man,
I pledge my homage till I die.

MARY

Ah, Joseph, husband, He is cold,
And we've no fire to warm Him by.

JOSEPH

King of all Kings, of field and wood,
Here, let me take You in my arm.
You might have had better if You would,
Than the breath of beasts to keep You warm.

MARY

Oh, Joseph, give Him back to me,
The Maker of man, and Savior mild.

JOSEPH
(*Giving the Babe to* MARY.)

I'll give Him to you, my sweet Mary,
The gentle beasts have warmed our Child.
(*The* SHEPHERDS *reach the crossing, where an* ANGEL
appears to them, from the transept, left.)

ANGEL

Shepherds kind,
Be not afraid
Of this star that you do see.
For this same morn
God's Son is born
In Bethlehem of a maiden free.

Hurry quickly, shepherds fair!
It is His will you see Him there,
Lying in a manger far from fine,
Though He has sprung from David's line.
    (*The* ANGEL *leaves as he came in. The* SHEPHERDS *approach and worship the Babe.*)

FIRST SHEPHERD

Hail, mother-maid and wife so mild!
We've found you as the Angel said.
I have no present for the Child,
But this, my pipe. Here, take it in Your hand.
It is my best, You understand.
And now, to honor Your glorious birth,
You shall have it, to bring You mirth.

SECOND SHEPHERD

Now hail, O Child, and mother, too!
These are indeed poor lodgings here,
Just as the Angel said they'd be.
Look, I'll give my cap to You,
And that will help You some, You see.
And so of weather You won't complain,
Not wind nor sun, hail, snow, or rain.

THIRD SHEPHERD

All hail, O Lord, O King of Bliss!
Your coming brings great happiness.
Here, take my mittens for Your pleasure.
I cannot offer other treasure.

MARY

Now shepherds, kind, I thank you so
For coming here,
To my sweet Son I'll pray,
That you may know
His blessed cheer
At your last day.

(*The* SHEPHERDS *go down the nave, singing*:)
(*Song*)
Down from heaven, from heaven so high,
Of angels there came a great company,
With mirth and joy and great solemnity.
They sang terli terlow;
So merrily the shepherds their pipes can blow.

(*The* CHOIR *sings* Glory, Glory to God in the Highest *as* MARY *and* JOSEPH *adore the Babe. Then the* CHOIR *forms a living curtain before the scene, and* MARY *and* JOSEPH *slip out.*)

The Innocents

CHARACTERS:

Mary	Second King
Joseph	Third King
Herod	An Angel
Messenger	First Knight
First King	Second Knight

Three Women

THE SCENE: *

The stage is bare except for a representation of the cattle shed and manger, which are placed upstage center. MARY, JOSEPH and the CHILD remain in tableau in this area throughout the play. The remainder of the action takes place in the neutral areas below and to left and right of this tableau. No scenery is required for the settings other than the manger, and the characters may come and go as they are needed. At the beginning of the play, HEROD enters to downstage center and speaks to the audience.

[*Playing time: 20 minutes*]

HEROD

(*Enters and advances to the center of the stage.*)

Prepare, you simple folk, to be astounded,
I'm the greatest King that ever existed!

* The characterization of Herod indicates that this play should be done in the recreation room rather than in the church proper.

Heaven and Hell by me were compounded;
My power and might cannot be resisted.
Both God and Magog by me were confounded,
Their bones with my shining sword I sundered,
So all the wide world was amazed and wondered.

Yes, I am the cause of this thunder and lightning;
It's my fury that hurls them at terra firma,
Making a roar that is certainly frightening;
And even the earth is afraid to murmur.
When I shake this bright sword with anger, watch out!
All the whole world, from the north to the south,
Will be smashed and destroyed at a word from my mouth.

To recite the whole tale of my majesty
Would take too long for a tongue to tell!
For the whole of the East is my realm, you see.
I am Prince of Purgatory, Captain of Hell!
And the traitors down there take orders from me,
To vanquish my foes and to smash them to clay;
At a wink of my eye, they would vanish away!

Just look at my aspect, the pride of a nation,
As bright as the sun at the height of the day!
What could possibly give you more inspiration
Than to look on my person, so handsome and gay,
And gorgeously garbed in the height of fashion?
He who could look all day long at my countenance
Would never require material sustenance.

Yes, I am King Herod of fame and renown,
Before whom the princes of earth all bow down!

And therefore, my Herald and trusty right hand,
Warn every port that no ships may anchor,
No alien strangers may pass through my land
Unless they pay toll—or they'll feel my rancor!
So hurry forth, I say,
For those who will not pay
Shall hang and not be buried!
There is no mercy in King Herod.

MESSENGER

Lord and Master, I hasten
To do as you think right.
I shall fly across your lands
As quick as light.

(*He goes out.*)

HEROD

Now my kingdom shall be searched
Every place, most carefully!
Any villains brought to me
Will regret their villainy.

(HEROD *exits and the* THREE KINGS *appear one at a time.*)

FIRST KING
(*Seeing the star.*)

Now blessed be God for this sweet sign!
The star that is to be my guide!
For He has come among us now,
As all the sages prophesied.

They said there would be born a child,
Coming out of Jesse's seed,

To save mankind that has been lost.
He comes in answer to our need.

I'll worship Him with all my heart,
Divine Creator, Man and God,
For as the Prophets have foretold
He saves us with His own sweet blood.

I pray that He may grant me grace,
By the star I see above,
To bring me safely to the Presence
Of His gentle, holy love.

SECOND KING
(*Entering.*)

I have never seen this place,
I'm sure I must have gone astray.
O God, Who fashioned man on earth,
Send me guidance on my way.

I think I see the fair, bright star,
Symbol of the tiny Child,
Come to set all mankind free,
Born of a mother undefiled.

I'll go on until I find Him
To worship Him is my intent.
Ah, there I see another King!
His company may be God-sent.
(*He approaches the* FIRST KING.)
Hark, I pray of you, sir King,
Tell me where you're journeying.

FIRST KING

To find a new-born Child
Of whom the prophets speak.
The star above is God's
Own sign of Him I seek.

SECOND KING

I pray you, please permit me
To keep you company.
I bring Him frankincense
As sign of His Divinity.

(*The* THIRD KING *enters.*)

THIRD KING

I wander strange and devious ways
Over mountain, dale and hill.
O King of Kings, I've gone astray;
Send me guidance, if You will.

Ah, there, far off, I see a sight
Bringing news of joy and mirth,
A child appearing in a star!
Has Our Saviour come to earth?

There I see two other Kings—
Perhaps they'll keep me company;
I'll go and speak with them.

(*He approaches the* TWO KINGS.)

Hail, fair Kings, most cordially!

Good sirs, where are you going?

FIRST KING

To see a little Child, new-born,
Betokened by that star.

SECOND KING

To find Him we have sworn.

THIRD KING

I pray you humbly, sirs,
To let me go along this night.

THE KINGS
(*In unison.*)

And now we pray Almighty God
That we may see this precious sight!
(*The* KINGS *go out.* HEROD *enters with the* MESSENGER.)

MESSENGER

Hail, most mighty Lord.
How wise was your command!
Three strange Kings have come
This night into your land.

HEROD

And what are they doing here in my country?

MESSENGER

They are seeking a king, a child new-born.

HEROD

How old is the child?

MESSENGER

Not twelve days yet.

HEROD

So young?

MESSENGER

Yes, so they described him this morn.

HEROD

Then bring them before me on pain of death,
And get on your way. They must appear
Before they have left my country behind.
Make sure that you bring all three of them here.
(*As the messenger starts to go.*)

And ask in Jerusalem more of the child,
But see that you speak with caution and care,
For we must be crafty and full of guile
To deceive the three kings in this affair.

MESSENGER

Lord, I am ready to do as you say,
I serve you as my Lord and King.

HEROD

At once then, hasten on your way!
And see that you are not too bold.
Commend me, too, to young and old.
(*The* THREE KINGS, *returning, are saluted by the* MES-
SENGER.)

MESSENGER

Hail, Sir Kings and noble lords!
Herod, King of all this land,
Summons you to speak with him,
And waits your coming close at hand.

FIRST KING

We obey, and gladly, too.
We will be pleased indeed to speak
With him; so come, my brothers—
He may tell us where to seek.

(*The* MESSENGER *leads them to* HEROD.)

MESSENGER

Here Lord, are the Kings;
I gave them your message.

HEROD

Welcome to all of you, gentle kings.
Don't be dismayed by my dazzling visage.

Sir Kings, a star, I understand,
Has guided you into my land.
And you have found a wondrous cheer
In admiration of its light.
Therefore, I beg you heartily here.
To tell me all about your quest.
How long since you first saw this sight?

FIRST KING

Sir King, it's been twelve days tonight,
Since first the star appeared in the west.

HEROD

There is no more to say then, brothers,
But keep to your journey with might and main,
And when you return, come back this way, too,
And tell me your news, so I, too, may gain.

You shall be honored my country through,
And banquet with me in friendship mild.
Then I, myself, shall worship the child.

SECOND KING

Sir, we'll obey your slightest command.
May He Who rules in everything
Show us the safest road, so we
May cross your land in peace, Sir King.

HEROD

And travel as leisurely as you wish.
Here is a passport you can use,
Good for a hundred days in my realm;
With this you may go wherever you choose.

THIRD KING

Farewell, then, mighty, exalted king.
We shall continue with our task.

HEROD

Farewell, and know that while I live
Whatever you wish is yours to ask.

(*The* THREE KINGS *go out.*)
There go three careless, foolish kings.

They've acted most unwisely here.
My purpose is to kill all three
The day they reappear.
Whoever goes against my laws,
No matter what his rank may be,
I shall destroy immediately.

(HEROD *goes out and the* THREE KINGS *reappear.*)

FIRST KING

O blessed God, in all Your might,
Where is the star that gave us light?

SECOND KING

Let us kneel down and pray to God
That he, in His magnificence,
Will lead us to the Child,
And so reward our diligence.

THIRD KING

Ah, there I see the star appear;
I'm sure the place we seek is here.

(*The* THREE KINGS *enter the place where the* CHILD *is lying beside* MARY.)

FIRST KING

Hail Lord, long-waited and long-sought!
Hail God and Man united!
Maker of all things from naught,
Although so poor you're lying here,
I bring a cup of gold to You,
A symbol that You have no peer.

SECOND KING

Hail to Your magnificence!
As symbol of divinity,
I bring You now a cup of incense,
Offered in humility.

THIRD KING

Hail, O long awaited Lord!
I offer You a cup of myrrh.
It represents mortality,
To show, O Saviour, You'll endure
Your death for us upon the tree.

MARY

God's blessings on you for this deed,
And the kindness of your thought.
And may God guard your journey home,
Remembering the gifts you brought.
                    (*The* KINGS *withdraw.*)

FIRST KING

And now, Sir Kings, we must return
To see King Herod, as we're bound.

SECOND KING

Yes, truly brothers; yet—first I must rest,
Before we tell him what we've found.

THIRD KING

And so must I. Let's all lie down
And rest a while upon the ground.

FIRST KING

I think that course is wise—we will.
And may the grace of that sweet Child
Protect us from all ill.
(*They lie down and fall asleep. An* ANGEL *appears.*)

ANGEL

Sir Jaspar, King of Taurus!
Balthasar, King of Araby!
And Melchor, King of Aginare!
I have been sent to warn you three.
Beware of Herod! Go the western way!
And you shall live at home in fame,
And die assured a greater glory.
In God's own name, I so proclaim!
(*The* ANGEL *leaves.*)

FIRST KING

I pray you, Kings, awake! Rejoice!
I dreamt I heard an Angel's voice.

SECOND KING

My brother, yes, your words are true!
He spoke our names; I heard him, too.

THIRD KING

He bade us go the western way,
For fear that Herod might betray
Us when we come.

FIRST KING

We'll do it then.
May that sweet Child show us the way.

Farewell then, fairest friends of all,
And thanked be Jesus for His grace,
That He, although we live apart,
Brought us together in this place.

We made our humble presentation.
To Him, the holy Son of God,
So we might earn our own salvation.
We may be glad indeed that we
Have carried out this sweet oblation.

SECOND KING
(*Bowing*)

Farewell to you, Sir Jaspar, brother,
Most worthy King of Taurus far.
I bow to you as well, Balthasar,
We never will forget the star.

Nor Him! I thank Him evermore
Who made us meet upon that hill.
We can go home with hearts rejoicing
In our obedience to His will.

THIRD KING

Now since we three must leave each other
For fear of Herod's angry hand,
Farewell, my friends, each cherished brother,
Each must return to his own land.

And He that brought us all together
Until our gifts to Him were given,

Grant us His grace to meet again,
Before His throne in heaven.

(*The* THREE KINGS *leave in different directions. The*
MESSENGER *enters, running, to* HEROD.)

MESSENGER

All hail, most mighty king of worth!
All hail, maintainer of the peace!
All hail, O greatest knight on earth!
All hail, you paragon of men!
The kings you sent to find the Child,
Who should have come to you again,
Went home another way, my lord,
And have escaped your vengeful sword.

HEROD

Another way! Another way!
Have those false traitors dared confound
King Herod? I will kill them all!
I stamp! I stare! I whirl around!

I rant! I rave! I'm going mad!
Such plots! How could the villains hatch them?
I'll burn them at the stake for certain!
I'll hang them all—if I can catch them.
            (*He storms up and down.*)
Aiee, I'll kill that rascal Child!
And all who follow Him, I'll rout!
Sir Knights, what do you think of this?
That I should send my soldiers out

To kill all children for this deed?
And others, if they fear to die,

Shall bow to Herod, as of old;
They'll offer me their wealth and gold.
They will not dare deny!

FIRST KNIGHT

My liege and lord! Oh, mighty Herod!
Your words go much against my will!
It is a shame to murder children.
I will not counsel you to kill.

SECOND KNIGHT

Well said, my friend. I am agreed.
Take care, King Herod! Stay your hand!
The murder of these little children
Will cause rebellion in your land.

HEROD

Rebellion? Rebellion! *Aieee! Aiee!*
      (*He storms up and down again.*)
Oh, villains, wretches! Plague upon you!
See that you carry out my will!
Or I shall hang you on the gallows,
By Mohammed's beard, I swear I shall!

FIRST KNIGHT

Oh, cruel King, since you demand it,—
And we must follow your decree—
All children of that age shall die!
I'll seek them out relentlessly!

SECOND KNIGHT

And I will swear upon your sword,
The children that I find I'll kill;

Till all the mothers weep and moan
When they behold my shining steel.
> (*They swear on* HEROD'S *sword.*)

HEROD

Go forth and do what you have sworn,
And work my will by day and night,
Kill every child that has been born
And when the children all are dead,
Then bring them here before my sight.
> (HEROD *and the* KNIGHTS *go out. An* ANGEL *appears
> and speaks to* MARY *and* JOSEPH.)

ANGEL

Mary and Joseph, I bring to you
A message from your God.
Go forth to Egypt this very morn,
And take with you the King, new-born.
Beware the wrath of Herod!
> (*The* ANGEL *leaves.*)

JOSEPH

My Mary, hurry and arise!
We must obey the good Lord's will,
Just as the Angel bade us now;
King Herod means to do us ill.

MARY

Oh yes, my husband, let us go
To Egypt now with humble hearts.
God grant us grace we come there safe,
And find a home in foreign parts.

(MARY *and* JOSEPH *go out, and* THREE WOMEN *enter with their* CHILDREN *in their arms. They are singing:*)

WOMEN *

Lully, lulla, O little, tiny child;
Bye, bye, lully, lullay, O little, tiny child;
Bye, bye, lully, lullay!

FIRST WOMAN

Oh, sisters two,
How may we do
For to preserve this day
This poor youngling
For whom we do sing,
Bye, bye, lully, lullay?

SECOND WOMAN

Herod, the king,
In his raging,
Charged he has this day
His men of might
In his own sight
All young children to slay.

THIRD WOMAN
(*Singing.*)

Oh, woe is me,
Poor child for thee,
Ever to mourn away
For your parting
Neither say nor sing,
Bye, bye, lully, lullay.

* For music to *Lully Lullay*, see p. 272.

The Innocents

THE THREE

Lully, lulla, O little, tiny child;
Bye, bye, lully, lullay, O little, tiny child;
Bye, bye, lully, lullay.

FIRST WOMAN

My sweet, the apple of my eye,
I rock him softly in my arms
So he'll not cry.

SECOND WOMAN

That Babe that's born in Bethlehem,
The tide of villainy will stem.

THIRD WOMAN

The Lord of Lords have mercy on us!
My little child, be still, be still!
For Herod has sworn with angry words,
That all the children he shall kill.
(The KNIGHTS *enter.)*

FIRST KNIGHT

Here, you wives of Bethlehem,
What's in your arms? We want to see.
If they are boys, they die today.
It is King Herod's royal decree.

SECOND KNIGHT

We shall kill each mother's son;
We dare not spare a single one.

FIRST WOMAN

Oh, gentle knights, I beg of you,
That you'll not shame your chivalry.
Have pity on my child,
In his sweet purity.
You know it would be dreadful murder
To slay or harm an innocent
Who never dreamed of wrong.
Oh, will you not relent?
       (*The* TWO KNIGHTS *look at each other guiltily.*)

SECOND KNIGHT
       (*Pulling himself together.*)
We must, though we were twice as loath.
We must, or we are traitors to our oath!
       (*The* KNIGHTS *draw their swords. Music swells mourn-*
       fully as the WOMEN *run out, pursued by the* KNIGHTS.
       The stage is empty for a moment. The WOMEN *can*
       be heard lamenting. Silence. The KNIGHTS *re-enter,*
       each carrying the swaddled form of a dead child.)

FIRST KNIGHT

How can a mortal bear the cry
Of women with their children slain?
It is a great and monstrous stain
On chivalry throughout this land!
And many men for this may die.
The awful wrong that we have done
Will be revenged on every one.

SECOND KNIGHT

O friend, the blood that we have spilt
Is not on us, but on the king,

For it is he must bear the guilt
Who was the cause of this great sin.
Now we must bring the dead to Herod
And show the dreadful sight to him.
(*They take the dead to* HEROD.)

FIRST KNIGHT

King Herod, look, that you may see
The children slain by your decree.

SECOND KNIGHT

Yes, Majesty, we've done your will.
No man can say that we've done ill.
(*The* MESSENGER *enters, running.*)

MESSENGER

Herod, King! I've news for you!
All you've done is come to nought;
For fled to Egypt is the Child,
The Child that you have sought!

HEROD

Fled to Egypt? He's escaped!
The Book of Prophecy was right!
All my power is put to scorn;
A King of overwhelming might,
A greater King than I, is born!
(*The* CHOIR *begins a hymn of praise in which the congregation joins, as* HEROD *and his followers leave the scene dejectedly.*)

The Second Shepherds Play

CHARACTERS:

First Shepherd   Mak
Second Shepherd   Gill
Third Shepherd   An Angel
              Mary

THE SCENE: *

The stage represents three places: the field of the
SHEPHERDS, the home of MAK, and a cattle shed on
the outskirts of Bethlehem. For a further description
of this scene, see staging notes, pp. 255 and 256.
[*Playing time*: *30 minutes*.]

FIRST SHEPHERD
(*Enters alone.*)

Lord, but this weather is cold!
And with these thin clothes
I'm nearly numb.
So long have I napped,
My legs they fold,
My fingers are chapped.

---

* Because of the extreme amount of secular material in this play, it
should not be performed in the church proper, but rather in the recreation room, where a stage, if it does not exist already, can easily be
improvised.

I've reason enough to be glum,
For I'm all wrapped
In sorrow.
Tempest and storm, east and west,
Woe to him who never has rest,
Midday or morrow.

Yes, we poor shepherds
Who walk the moor,
In faith, we're nearly
Turned out our door.
No wonder it stands
That we are poor,
For the wealth of our lands
Is fallow as the floor,
As you can see.
We're so burdened with tax and tithe
That on the rack we're made to writhe
By the nobility.

That's the way they steal our rest!
I curse them every one!
These greedy landlords take the best,
And leave us poor with none.
That, men say, is for the best.
We find it isn't so.
It's thus we free men are oppressed
Until we're ready to let go
Our lives.
And that's the way they hold us under.
Now isn't it a nine-day wonder
A shepherd survives?

Here comes an upstart,
As proud as can be.
He must borrow my cart,
"And your plow," says he.
And before he'll depart,
I must give them to him,
Or he'll make me smart
For his every whim
By night and day.
And I must hand over everything,
For it would surely be better to swing
Than send him away.

It does no good to walk,
Like this, alone,
And take it out in talk,
To weep and moan.
I'll go and join my flock,
And play a little tune,
And sit upon a rock,
And wait for the moon;
For if my friends are true to me
They'll come and keep me company,
And very soon.

>   (*He sits down with his back to the audience. The*
>   SECOND SHEPHERD *enters. He does not see the* FIRST
>   SHEPHERD.)

SECOND SHEPHERD

Almighty God, look after us!
What does this blizzard mean?

Why does the world attack us thus?
The like was never seen!
Oh, Lord, the weather's full of spite,
The cutting wind is keen.
The bitter frost has such a bite,
It's never been so mean,
And that's no jest!
Now dry, now wet, now snow, now sleet;
When your shoes are freezing to your feet
It isn't for the best.

But even further, then:
Wherever I go,
I see we married men
Are full of woe.
Trouble is ours again and again;
It's always so.
Lucky Copelia, our little hen,
Runs to and fro
And cackles.
But if she begins to croak or cluck,
Then woe to our unhappy cock,
For he's in the shackles.

All men that are wed
Have nothing their own.
They're sore bestead,
They sigh and groan.
God knows they are led
A terrible life.
Not a word is said

Except by the wife.
No use to hide it,
This is the lesson that I have found:
Woe to the man who in marriage is bound,
For he must abide it.

(*He addresses the audience.*)
So, young men, be loath,
Before you are caught,
Of taking the oath;
And think in your thought,
"Had I known," is a thing
That serves you for nought.
For a wedding ring
Is dearly bought
With strife.
And a man may catch in a careless hour
What first seemed sweet, but will savour sour
All his life.

Before I ever read an epistle,
I had one by my fire
As sharp as a thistle,
As rough as a briar;
She has brows like a bristle,
A vinegar face!
If she once wets her whistle,
She can sing apace
Her *Pater Noster*.
She's as great as a hall, and most of it gall!
I swear by Him that died for us all:
I wish I had run till I'd lost her.

FIRST SHEPHERD
(*Interrupts him, slapping his back.*)

Man! Look where you stand!
You act like you're blind!

SECOND SHEPHERD
(*Startled.*)

The Fiend take your hand,
Before and behind!
Have you seen our friend, Dall?

FIRST SHEPHERD

Yes, down below, I heard him call.
Stand still . . .

SECOND SHEPHERD

But why?

FIRST SHEPHERD

We'll play a game.
We'll hide.

SECOND SHEPHERD

He'll find us all the same.
(*Enter the* THIRD SHEPHERD, *a boy*.)

THIRD SHEPHERD

God give me speed,
And Saint Nicholas!
That's what I need.
It is worse than it was!
Let him who can take heed

And let the world pass!
It is fearful indeed,
As brittle as glass,
And slick as an eel.
This world has never been so before
With terrible marvels, more and more!
It makes me reel!

Never since Noah's flood
Have such floods been seen;
Winds and rains so rude,
And storms so keen!
Some stammered, some stood
With doubtful mien.
Now God turn all to good.
I say what I mean,
For ponder:
These floods in the pasture and in the town
If they go on, they'll make us all drown!
Now, wouldn't that be a wonder?

We that walk in the nights,
Our cattle to keep,
We see sudden sights
While other men sleep.
                    (*He sees the others.*)
Oh, I feel my heart fall!
There I see two scoundrels peep.
They're the ones who know it all.
                    (*He turns to go away.*)
I will get my sheep
And leave.

(He hesitates.)
But wait! I shouldn't leave in spite,
But satisfy my appetite,
Or I'll grieve.

(He turns back. The other two SHEPHERDS *come toward him.)*
God give you Grace,
Oh, master mine.
Is this the place
Where we drink and dine?

FIRST SHEPHERD

Why, curse you, knave,
You lazy swine!

SECOND SHEPHERD

Oh, let him rave!
(He brings out food and he and the FIRST SHEPHERD *sit down to eat. The* SECOND SHEPHERD *continues talking to the* THIRD SHEPHERD. *Teasingly:)*
Just take your time,
And let *us* have some.
You've got to learn to be quick on your feet
And though you are late, you may still get to eat—
If we leave you a crumb.

THIRD SHEPHERD

Such servants as I,
Who sweat and slave,
Our bread is dry,
And that's why I "rave."

We're often hard at work
When master is asleep,
And yet he'll always shirk
On our food and keep.
And still
While we are toiling in the mire,
The master squanders all our hire,
And pays us when he will.

(*He sits down to eat with the other* SHEPHERDS.)
But here's my pledge, master:
For the food you give,
I shall only work hereafter,
As well as I live.
I'll do but little good,
And in between I'll play,
For I never had enough food
To last me a working day
In the field.
So why should I work when I can play?
As the saying is, "The lowest pay,
The lightest yield."

FIRST SHEPHERD

Indeed you're brash,
My foolish friend,
To ask for more cash,
When I've little to spend.

SECOND SHEPHERD

Peace, boy, I say!
Let's have no more jangling,

Or you'll rue the day
That you started wrangling
With us.
Where are our sheep, boy?

THIRD SHEPHERD

Early this morn
They all were standing in the corn.
I left them thus.

They have plenty of food,
They cannot go wrong.

FIRST SHEPHERD

That's right.
                      (He shivers.)
           By the rood,
These nights are long.
Before we go I would
We'd all sing a song.

SECOND SHEPHERD
(Putting the remainder of the food away.)

That idea is good.
Let's sing it out strong!

THIRD SHEPHERD

I'm in favor.

FIRST SHEPHERD

Let me sing in the baritone key!

SECOND SHEPHERD

And I the tenor.

THIRD SHEPHERD

Then the bass falls to me.
Let's hear you quaver.

ALL THREE SHEPHERDS *
(*Singing*)

As I rode out this past midnight
Of three jolly shepherds I caught a sight;
And all about their fold a star shone bright.

They sang, "Terli terlow,
So merrily the shepherds their pipes can blow."

(MAK *enters at the other side of the stage with a cloak
drawn over his rough shepherd clothes.*)

MAK
(*To himself.*)

Oh, Lord of mighty fame—
That made both moon and stars,
And more than I can name—
Your bounty has been sparse.
My very brain is lame
From fate's rude shocks and jars.
It's such unhappy shame
To see your children's tears
Each day.

FIRST SHEPHERD
(*Stands.*)

Who's that wailing man so poor?

* For music to *Terli Terlow*, see pp. 271 and 272.

MAK

(*Seeing the* FIRST SHEPHERD.)

There's a man that walks the moor
And comes my way.

SECOND SHEPHERD

(*Rises and goes to* MAK.)

Where are you going, Mak?
What news do you bring?

THIRD SHEPHERD

(*Rises.*)

Is that one back?
Then watch everything!
(*He wraps his cloak tightly about himself.*)

MAK

(*To the* SECOND SHEPHERD.)

I'm not this Mak!
I serve the King.
So change your tack,
And my praises sing,
You scurvy ram!
Fie on you, and go you hence!
Away! I must have reverence!
Who do you think I am?

FIRST SHEPHERD

Why do you act in this wise?
Why, Mak, it's wrong!

SECOND SHEPHERD

Yes, Mak, why the disguise?
We've known you too long.

THIRD SHEPHERD

Don't throw sand in honest eyes!
I'd hang you for a song!

MAK

I'll complain about your lies,
And you shall feel the thong
At a word from me,
When I tell of the insolent jibes you make!

FIRST SHEPHERD

Don't try to fool us! Devil take
Your villainy!

SECOND SHEPHERD

The Devil seize your back!
I'll lend you a blow!
                    (*He strikes* MAK.)

THIRD SHEPHERD

Don't you know me, Mak?
Well, I'll remind you—so!
                    (*He draws back to strike* MAK.)

MAK

Why, God be with you three!
I didn't know you from afar.
You are good company.

The Second Shepherds Play 7 1

FIRST SHEPHERD

Well, now do you know who you are?

SECOND SHEPHERD

Your joke can keep!
What will men think of this situation?
You out late, with your reputation
For stealing sheep!

MAK

Yet I am true as steel,
As all men know;
But a sickness I feel
That lays me low.
My stomach's not well.
It hurts me so.

THIRD SHEPHERD

The Fiend never fell
In the road, you know.

MAK

Therefore,
I swear by every mortal sin,
I haven't eaten as much as a pin
For a month and more!

FIRST SHEPHERD

And how is your wife?
Yes, how is she?

MAK

She leads a good life!
Much better than me!

Has a house full of young,
And she drinks well, too,
And works with her tongue!
That's all she'll do.
I swear it's true!
It's just when she eats that her tongue is mild,
And each year she brings forth another child,
And some years two!

SECOND SHEPHERD
(*Yawning.*)

I'm sure none in the shire
Is so dead for sleep.
For a penny's hire
I'd forget my sheep.

THIRD SHEPHERD
(*Shivering.*)

I wish we'd a fire,
The cold is so deep.

FIRST SHEPHERD

I've run through the mire
Till I'm ready to weep.
You watch and take care.

SECOND SHEPHERD

No. I'll lie down. I must have some rest.

THIRD SHEPHERD

I'm just as good a man as the best;
I'll have my share.

The sheep are secure
As long as Mak is with us.
And just to make sure,
We'll keep him thus.
Lie down between us, Mak;
We'll keep you from the weather.

MAK

I fear I'll hold you back
If you want to talk together.

THIRD SHEPHERD

No fear!

MAK

As you will. From my top to my toe
    (*As the others push him down.*)
I commend myself to your hands, Pontius Pilatio.
    (*The others have pushed him down on the ground.*)
I'll lie here.
    (*The others lie down closely on either side of him.
    When the others are asleep,* MAK *rises.*)

MAK

Now is the time for a man
With an empty hold,
As slyly as he can
To slip into a fold,
And nimbly to worry
One out. Not too bold;
For he might be sorry
If it were told

At the end.
Now is the time when a clever man strikes,
If he would live as well as he likes
And has little to spend.

*(He pretends to be a magician and draws a circle on
the ground around the sleeping men.)*

About you a circle,
As round as a moon,
Till I've done what I will—
Till it be noon.
So you lie stone still
Until I'm through;
And when you wake I'll show my skill
At telling lies to you.

(Waving his hands in the air over their heads.)

The Devil's pact:
I lift my hands high over thee!
Out go your eyes! You cannot see!—
Now to act!

(The SHEPHERDS *begin to snore.)*

They sleep like rocks
With never a turn.
I never kept flocks,
But now I'll learn.
Though the sheep take fright
Yet I'll come near.

*(He goes to the edge of the stage and begins coaxing
the sheep which are just off-stage and thus cannot be
seen by the audience.)*

Come, little sheep! Ah, yes, that's right!
This will mean good cheer,
The end of sorrow.

(He goes off-stage and we hear him, but cannot see him.)

Fat sheep, good fleece, a fine beast, I dare say!
I'll pay for the animal some fine day.

(He comes in, carrying the sheep.)

This one I will borrow.

(He crosses to his home.)

Hey, Gill, are you in?
Get us some light!

GILL

(Who is inside their home.)

Who makes such a din
At this time of night?
I've sat down to spin!
I wouldn't get up, no not for a sight!
I wouldn't get up, a penny to win!
Come back when it's light!
So fares
A housewife, if you please;
She never has a minute's ease
From trivial cares.

MAK

(Knocking on the door.)

Open the door and come on out.
I bring you meat!

GILL

Draw the latch yourself, you lout!
   (MAK enters the house, and she sees what he is carrying.)
Ah, come in, my sweet!

MAK

That's not the song you sang
While I was out there, cold.

GILL

No, and you are like to hang
Long before you're old!

MAK

Go away!
When I need it, I can get
More than those who work and sweat
All the day.

(*He shows her the sheep.*)
This is what I bring
To satisfy our need.

GILL

It would be an awful thing
If they hang you for the deed!

MAK

I've stood much harder blows
And gotten away.

GILL

Yes the pitcher often goes
To water, as they say
In every land,
But at last it comes home broken.

MAK

I know the words, but let them not be spoken.
Come, lend a hand.

I would he were dead;
I want to eat.
I'm tired of bread;
I want some meat.

GILL

If they come before he's sped,
And hear the sheep bleat—

MAK

I'll be the one who's bled!
I can feel the clammy winding-sheet!
                    (*He begins to tremble.*)
Go bar the door!

GILL

Yes, if they sneak up behind your back—

MAK

I'd be caught by all the pack!
            (*He runs and peeks out of the door.*)
The Devil give warning before!

GILL

A good trick I have spied
Since you have none.
Give him here. We'll hide
The sheep till they are gone.

(MAK *gives her the sheep.*)

In my cradle he'll abide.

(GILL *puts the sheep in the cradle.*)

You let me alone,
And I shall lie beside
In childbed and groan.

MAK

Well said!
And I shall say you've given birth
To a son tonight.

GILL

On all this earth
Was never bred
Such a good device!
  (*She ties a baby bonnet on the sheep and covers it
  with a blanket.*)
It's a far cast;
Yet a woman's advice
Helps at the last.
They may come in a trice,
So go back there fast!
  (GILL *crawls into her bed next to the cradle.*)

MAK

The plan must suffice,
Else it blows a cold blast.
I will go sleep.
  (*He leaves his home and returns to the* SHEPHERDS.)
I'll slip in among them.
  (*He resumes his place.*)
  Here I'll lie

As if indeed it had never been I
That stole their sheep.

(*There is a short pause during which* MAK *snores*
loudly, then the FIRST *and* SECOND SHEPHERDS *awaken.*)

FIRST SHEPHERD
(*Sits up, bewildered.*)

It's the Resurrection!
Grab hold of my hand.
I'm broken in sections;
I cannot stand!
My senses spin,
My foot is tinglin'!
What land are we in?
We lay down in England.

SECOND SHEPHERD
(*Stretching.*)

Ah—*eee!*
What a good sleep! I'm fresh as an eel!
And cheerful, too. And so light I feel
As a leaf on a tree!

(*He and the* FIRST SHEPHERD *stand up.*)

THIRD SHEPHERD
(*Awakes.*)

Blessings on all here-in!
My body is quaking;
My heart is out of my skin;
My hands are shaking.
Who makes all this din?
My head is breaking!

Where is the door I came in?
Oh! Friends! It's time to be waking!
We're missing one!
Where's Mak? He's the one we miss.

FIRST SHEPHERD

We were up first.

SECOND SHEPHERD
I can promise you this:

He isn't gone.

THIRD SHEPHERD
(*Standing up.*)

I dreamed he was wrapped
In a wolf-skin.

FIRST SHEPHERD

So many are apt
To be—within.

THIRD SHEPHERD

I thought, while we napped,
He had gotten a gin
And gone out and trapped
A sheep with no din.

SECOND SHEPHERD

Be still!
It's only a dream, I swear by the rood!

FIRST SHEPHERD

Now Almighty God turn all to good,
If it be Your will!

(*They awaken* MAK.)

SECOND SHEPHERD

Rise, Mak, for shame!
You're lying too long!

MAK

(*Sits up and rubs his eyes elaborately.*)

Now, by His holy name!
Who am I among?
What's this, by my fame?
I'm limp as a thong.—
Yet I'm sure I'm the same.
Oooh! My neck's twisted wrong.
Oh, my head!

(*They help him to his feet.*)

Thank you. I had such a terrible dream,
I'm sure that you must have heard me scream.
I'm nearly dead!

I thought Gill began to groan
And carry on so sad;
And soon, with a terrible moan,
She gave birth to another lad
To fill out our flock.
And I wasn't too glad
To have another to rock
Besides the ones I had.
Oh, my head!
A house full of young ones to drive you wild!
Woe is the man who has many a child
And has little bread!

I must go home, by your leave,
To Gill—if it is as I thought.

(*He holds out his arms.*)

I pray you, look up my sleeve
To see I have stolen nought.
I wouldn't want you to grieve;
And I wouldn't take from you aught.

    (MAK *leaves them and goes to his home.*)

THIRD SHEPHERD
(*As he is leaving.*)

Go on! You were born to thieve!
Let's see what he may have wrought
This morn.
Let's count our sheep and see they're all there.

FIRST SHEPHERD

And when we're through, let's meet.

SECOND SHEPHERD

      But where?

THIRD SHEPHERD

At the crooked thorn.
  (*All the* SHEPHERDS *leave the stage.* MAK *arrives at his home.*)

MAK
(*Knocking.*)

Open the door! Is anyone here?
Will you open it soon?

GILL

What a din in my ear!
Go, walk with the moon!

MAK

Ah, Gill, what cheer?
> (*Pause. He gets no answer.*)

It's your Mak, you loon!

GILL

> (*In the house.*)

Must I always hear
The same old tune?
Can't you wait?
> (*She gets out of bed and comes and opens the door.*)

Who does the work, the waking? Who comes, who goes?
Who does the brewing, the baking? Who sews up your
  hose?
What a fate!

Was the game well played
With the shepherds, Mak?

MAK

The last word that they said
When I turned my back
Was that they were afraid
They must count their pack.
I hope they'll be paid
When they find their lack.
What a shame!
It'll go the way it always goes;
They'll think of me, and I suppose
It's me they'll blame.

Then you must do as you said.

GILL

I'm ready to do it.
        (*She goes to the cradle and looks at the sheep.*)
I've swaddled him,—even his head;
There's nothing to it.
I put him in the baby's bed.
I hope we may not rue it.
I'll lie and moan till they're misled.

MAK

Don't overdo it.
        (GILL *crawls into bed again, and* MAK *tucks her in.*)

GILL

Now let them come,
Coll and his mates, and search the house!

MAK

They'll never find so much as a mouse,
If we play dumb.

GILL

Now hark for their call.
They'll come anon.
Make ready, now, all.
You must sing alone.
Sing lullay you shall,
For I must groan
And cry out by the wall
On Mary and John,
Louder and stronger!
Sing loud lullay when they come near.

I'll play my part well; you wait and hear,
Or trust me no longer.
> (MAK *goes to the door and watches for the* SHEPHERDS
> *who return and meet at the other side of the stage.*)

THIRD SHEPHERD

Ah, Coll, good morn!
Why aren't you asleep?

FIRST SHEPHERD

Alas, that I was born!
We've lost a fat sheep!
And I am all forlorn.

THIRD SHEPHERD

Ah, may the good Lord keep
Us from all scorn!

SECOND SHEPHERD

Ah, me, that wound is deep!

FIRST SHEPHERD

The shrew!
I've looked all over till I'm nearly blind!
I've searched the thickets, but couldn't find
My ewe!

THIRD SHEPHERD

Now, believe me, if you will,
By Saint Thomas of Kent,
Either Mak or Gill
Is behind this event!

FIRST SHEPHERD

Peace man, be still.
I saw when he went;
So you slander him ill.
You ought to repent
With speed.

SECOND SHEPHERD

Now as I live, and as I hope to see
The other world, I swear it must be he
Who did the deed!

THIRD SHEPHERD

Let's go drag him out of bed,
And quickly, forsooth!
I shall never eat bread
Till I know the truth!

FIRST SHEPHERD

Nor shall my thirst be fed
Until I meet him.

SECOND SHEPHERD

I will rest in no stead
Until *I* meet him!
Let's go!
We'll find out if we're right;
And we'll not sleep tonight
Until we know.

> (*The* SHEPHERDS *approach* MAK's *house. He sees them
> and warns* GILL *who begins to groan.* MAK *sits down
> by the cradle and sings* Sing Ivy.)

MAK *
(*Singing.*)

My father gave me an acre of land,
  Sing ovy, sing ivy,
My father gave me an acre of land,
  A bunch of green holly and ivy.

I harrowed it with a bramble bush,
  Sing ovy, sing ivy,
I harrowed it with a bramble bush,
  A bunch of green holly and ivy.

I sowed it with two peppercorns,
  Sing ovy, sing ivy,
I sowed it with two peppercorns,
  A bunch of green holly and ivy.

I rolled it with a rolling pin,
  Sing ovy, sing ivy,
I rolled it with a rolling pin,
  A bunch of green holly and ivy.

I reaped it with my little penknife,
  Sing ovy, sing ivy,
I reaped it with my little penknife,
  A bunch of green holly and ivy.

I stowed it in a mouse's hole,
  Sing ovy, sing ivy,
I stowed it in a mouse's hole,
  A bunch of green holly and ivy.

* For music to *Sing Ivy*, see p. 273.

I threshed it out with two beanstalks,
    Sing ovy, sing ivy,
I threshed it out with two beanstalks,
    A bunch of green holly and ivy.

I sent my rats to market with that,
    Sing ovy, sing ivy,
I sent my rats to market with that,
    A bunch of green holly and ivy.

My team of rats came rattling back,
    Sing ovy, sing ivy,
My team of rats came rattling back,
With fifty bright guineas and an empty sack,
    A bunch of green holly and ivy.

THIRD SHEPHERD

Listen to him hack!
Our friend tries to croon.

FIRST SHEPHERD

I never heard a voice crack
So clear out of tune.
Let's call him out.

SECOND SHEPHERD
(*Knocks on the door.*)

Mak! Open the door!

MAK
(*Stops singing.*)

What was that shout?
As loud as a roar,

And at night?
Who is it, I say?

THIRD SHEPHERD

Don't you know us?
(MAK *opens the door and the* THIRD SHEPHERD *puts his
foot in the crack.*)
Good day!

MAK

Oh, it's you. Well, as far as you may,
Speak soft, tread light

By a sick woman's bed,
Who's feverish and queasy.
I'd rather be dead
Than make her uneasy.

GILL

Get out of my house!
I'm sore bestead!
If you walked like a mouse
It would pound in my head
Like thunder!

FIRST SHEPHERD

Now tell us, Mak, how you are, if you may.

MAK

Why, what are you doing in town today
I wonder?
(*With exaggerated compassion.*)

You have walked through the mire.
You're wet to the skin!
I'll make you a fire
If you will come in.
                    (*The* SHEPHERDS *enter the house.*)
I would hire a nurse,
For there's trouble anew,
And much, much worse! —
My dream has come true!
This season
I have children and troubles enough, I think;
But as you brew, so must you drink,
That's only reason.
                    (*Solicitously.*)
I wish I could give you a little food.
Will you drink? You sweat.

SECOND SHEPHERD

No, neither will mend our mood,
Neither drink nor meat.

MAK

Why, sir! Is not everything good?

THIRD SHEPHERD

One of our sheep, as it ate,
Was stolen where it stood.
Our loss is great.

MAK

Sirs, drink and forget!
                    (*With elaborate righteousness.*)
Someone would have smarted, had I been there!

FIRST SHEPHERD

Well, Mak, there're some men think that you were;
And that has us upset.

SECOND SHEPHERD

Mak, some men state
That it must be you.

THIRD SHEPHERD

Either you or your mate,—
One of the two.

MAK

Now, if you suspect
Myself or my heart,
Come, show no respect!
Rip our house apart!
Go ahead!
If I have stolen any man's sheep,
Or Gill, my wife, has awakened from sleep
Since she went to bed,

As I'm as true as steel,
To God here I pray
            (*He points to the cradle.*)
That this be the first meal
I shall eat today!

FIRST SHEPHERD

Mak, for your own weal
You should know what they say:
He learns early to steal
Who cannot say nay.
        (*The* SHEPHERDS *begin to search the house.*)

GILL

I cannot sleep!
Out thieves! You've hearts like stones!
You've come to rob us!

MAK

                              Oh, hear how she groans!
Your hearts should weep!

GILL

You thieves! Get away!
Away from my child!

MAK

If you knew how she's suffered today,
Your hearts would be mild.
You do wrong, I say,
To act so wild.
You'll find nothing that way.
You've not been beguiled.

GILL

Ah, my middle!
I swear that if I've ever done
The thing you say, I'll eat my son
Who lies in the cradle!

MAK

Peace, woman, for God's pain!
And cry not so!
You torture your brain,
And fill mine full of woe!

SECOND SHEPHERD
(Returning from the search.)

Our sheep is slain!
I know it is so!

THIRD SHEPHERD
(Also returning.)

But we've looked in vain.
We may as well go,
For by Saint Kate,
I haven't found bone, and I haven't found flesh,
Not even salt meat, and much less fresh, —
But an empty plate!

(He stands by the cradle and looks scornfully from
MAK *to* GILL. *He sniffs suspiciously.)*
Though with people like this
You never could tell
If he's here, by my bliss,
As foul as they smell.

GILL

No, that's an injustice
I swear by my child!

FIRST SHEPHERD

We've gone amiss.
I think we're beguiled.

SECOND SHEPHERD

I fear we're undone.
(He, too, stands by the cradle and addresses MAK.*)*
I ask you, sir, is the child a boy?

MAK
(By the cradle. Worried.)

Why, yes, my friend, he is to our joy.
A son.

SECOND SHEPHERD
(Wants to shake hands with MAK *across the cradle.)*

Mak, friends will we be,
For we're all one.

MAK
(Backing away from the cradle and his hand.)

We! No, don't count on me,
For I'll have none.
Farewell, all three.
I'll be glad when you're gone.
  (The SHEPHERDS *leave.* MAK *breathes deeply with re-
  lief and goes to the cradle and pulls the blanket down.
  GILL gets out of bed and joins him. They laugh to-
  gether and admire the sheep.)*

THIRD SHEPHERD

Fair words may there be,
But love is there none,
I fear.

FIRST SHEPHERD

Did you give the child a little gift?

SECOND SHEPHERD

Not a thing.
                    I'll run back and do it swift.

THIRD SHEPHERD

Wait for me here.

(*The* THIRD SHEPHERD *returns to* MAK'S *house and
knocks on the door.* GILL *dives for her bed and groans
elaborately.* MAK *hurriedly covers the sheep and goes
to open the door.*)
Mak, don't take it ill.
I've come to make amends.

MAK

Nay, I've had my fill
Of you and your friends.
                 (*He tries to close the door.*)

THIRD SHEPHERD
        (*Putting his foot in the crack.*)

The child will not grieve,
The dear little joy,
So, please, by your leave,
        (*He forces his way into the room and goes to the
        cradle.*)
Let me offer your boy
A six-pence.

MAK

No, go away! Can't you see he's asleep?

THIRD SHEPHERD

He wants to play.

MAK
        If he wakes, he'll weep!
Get hence!

THIRD SHEPHERD

Let me give him a kiss;
I'll lift up the clout—
  (*He lifts the cloth and thinks the baby is deformed.*)
What the devil is this?
He has a long snout!
  (*The other* SHEPHERDS *who by now have also re-
turned and entered the house, press forward and look
at the baby.*)

FIRST SHEPHERD

He's as foul as a curse,
So ugly and queer!

SECOND SHEPHERD
  (*With a sly look at* GILL.)

You can't make a silk purse
From a sow's ear.
  (*Suddenly realizing that it is a sheep.*)
Ah, so!
He looks just exactly like our sheep!

THIRD SHEPHERD

Here, Gyb, let me look!

FIRST SHEPHERD
                    Yes, nature will creep
Where it cannot go.
  (*They lift the sheep out of the cradle.*)

SECOND SHEPHERD

A quaint trick, by the Lord,
And a far cast!
A genuine fraud!

THIRD SHEPHERD

And almost got past.
                    (*He looks at* GILL.)
Let's burn this bawd!
Let's bind her fast!
I shall applaud
When she hangs at last,
And no man mourns.
Just see how they've tied his four feet in the middle.
I have never seen such a sight in a cradle,—
A lad with horns!

MAK

Peace, I say! What!
Let me hear no more!
He was honestly got,
Yon woman him bore!

FIRST SHEPHERD

What's the devil's name?
"Mak"? He's Mak's heir.

SECOND SHEPHERD

Jest,—but all the same,
God give him care,
I say.

GILL

As pretty a child is he
As ever sat on a woman's knee.
And made a man gay.

THIRD SHEPHERD
(*Examining the sheep.*)

I know him by the earmark;
That's a good token.

MAK

I tell you, sirs, hark:
His nose was broken;
Afterwards I was told by a clerk
That he'd been bespelled.

FIRST SHEPHERD

This is a false work.
My anger will not be quelled!
Get a weapon!

GILL

He was taken by an elf when the clock struck twelve! —
I saw it, I tell you, I saw it myself, —
And so misshapen!

SECOND SHEPHERD

You two are right deft
From all that's been said.

THIRD SHEPHERD

Since they deny their theft,
Let's beat them dead!

MAK
(*Frightened.*)

You may chop off my head
If I trespass again.
I'll reform instead.

FIRST SHEPHERD

Sirs, to his pain
For this trespass
We'll not quarrel, nor argue, nor curse,
Fight him or chide. We'll do nothing worse
Than toss him in canvas!

(They get the blanket from GILL's *bed and toss* MAK
*in it while he squeals with fear. Then they return to
the field and the lights go down on the home of* MAK
and GILL *who leave the stage in the darkness.)*

FIRST SHEPHERD

*(After putting the sheep offstage, ostensibly leaving
it with the rest of the flock, returns to the others.)*
Lord, but I'm sore!
I could almost weep.
I can stand no more.
I have to sleep.

SECOND SHEPHERD

What a heavy sheep!
What a tossing chore!
I would like to sleep
Any place on the moor.

THIRD SHEPHERD

Now, I pray,
Let's lie down right here in the stubble.

FIRST SHEPHERD

I'm thinking of Mak.

THIRD SHEPHERD

Don't go borrowing trouble.
Just do as I say.

(*They lie down and fall asleep. An* ANGEL *appears and speaks to them. The star above the manger blazes forth.*)

ANGEL

Rise, Shepherds, redeemed!
For now He is born,
Who shall snatch from the Fiend
Mankind forlorn!

(*The* SHEPHERDS *awaken.*)

Yes, the Devil must yield
To Him who is born.
God is revealed
On this sacred morn!
Go east
To Bethlehem and see
Him in a manger, poor and free,
Between two beasts.

(*The* ANGEL *withdraws.*)

FIRST SHEPHERD

His voice had a beautiful ring,
As fine as any I have heard.
It is a wonderful thing
To hear God's word!

SECOND SHEPHERD

It's God's Son so good
Whom the angel named,

And the whole dark wood
With lightning flamed
So fair!

THIRD SHEPHERD

He spoke of a Child in Bethlehem far.

FIRST SHEPHERD

That is the meaning of yonder star.
Let us seek Him there.

SECOND SHEPHERD

"Bethlehem," he said.
That's where we belong.
I'm sore afraid
To tarry is wrong.

THIRD SHEPHERD

Be merry, not sad,
Of mirth is our song!
Now men can be glad
If their faith is strong
And bright.

FIRST SHEPHERD

No matter how wet and weary we be,
This Lady and Child we must see
Tonight.

SECOND SHEPHERD

Full glad may we be,
We abide the day

That Wonder to see
Who all things may!
Lord, well were me,
For once and for aye,
To kneel on my knee
Some word for to say
To that Child.
But the angel said He was laid
In a crib, and poorly arrayed,
So meek and mild.

FIRST SHEPHERD

Patriarchs that have been,
And prophets before,
They wished to have seen
That Child that is born.
They are gone full clean,
Their hope was forlorn.
But we shall see Him, I ween,
Before it is morn
As a token.
And when I see Him, I'm sure I shall feel
That I know full well, it is true as steel
What the prophets have spoken:

That He would appear
To men, poor as we are,
Announced to us here
By a song and a star.

SECOND SHEPHERD

It is very near;
Let us hurry apace.
                    (*They start toward the manger.*)

THIRD SHEPHERD

I am ready, no fear.
Let us enter the place
That is undefiled.
Lord, if it be Your will this day,
Show three unlettered men the way
To comfort Your Child.

(*They enter the stable in which are* MARY *and the*
CHRIST CHILD. *The* FIRST SHEPHERD *kneels before the*
BABE.)

FIRST SHEPHERD

Hail, comely and clean!
Hail, young Child!
Hail, Maker, I mean!
And hail, Maiden mild!
You have cursed, I ween,
The Devil so wild!
So false and unclean,
Now goes he beguiled.
Lo! He merries!
Lo, how He laughs, the sweet little thing!
A wonderful meeting!

(*He holds out a little bundle to the* CHILD.)

And look how I bring
You a bunch of cherries!

SECOND SHEPHERD
(*Kneels.*)

Hail, Sovereign Savior,
For whom we have sought!
Hail freely, Leaf and Flower,

Who all things has wrought!
Hail, full of favor,
Who made all from nought!
Hail! I kneel and I cower.
                    (*He holds out a little bird.*)
A bird have I brought
From afar.
Hail to You, sweet little Promised Boy!
At last You have come to us, Bringer of Joy!
Little Day-Star!

                    THIRD SHEPHERD
                    (*Kneels.*)

Hail, darling dear,
Full of Godhead!
I pray You, be near
When I have need.
Hail! Sweet is Your cheer!
My heart must bleed
To see You lie here
In these poor weeds
With never a penny.
                    (*He holds out a little ball.*)
Put out Your hand in answer to my call;
I bring You nothing but this ball.
Take it. You'll not have many.

                    MARY

The Father above,
Omnipotent,
Who out of His love,
His Son has sent

To save us all,
May He give us grace
From the sin of the fall
By the light of His face
Who to me is born!
May He keep you from woe!
I shall pray Him so,
Wherever you go
After this morn.

FIRST SHEPHERD

Farewell, Lady,
So fair to behold
With your Child on your knee!

SECOND SHEPHERD

But He lies so cold.
Ah, well is me,
We'll go with hearts bold!

THIRD SHEPHERD

Yes, now I can see
There's no more to be told
At this time.

(*The* SHEPHERDS *leave the manger.*)

FIRST SHEPHERD

What grace we have found!

SECOND SHEPHERD

Come! To sing we are bound!

THIRD SHEPHERD

Let us ring out the rhyme!
*(They go out singing a Christmas hymn in which the
audience joins.)*

St. Nicholas and the Scholars

CHARACTERS:

Old Man	*Second Scholar*
Old Woman	*Third Scholar*
First Scholar	*St. Nicholas*

THE SCENE: *

The scene represents the exterior and interior of a poor medieval home, that of the OLD MAN and his wife. Upstage left is the house, represented by a single wall with a door; the wall is left center, at right angles to the audience. In the area to its left are a table and chair, and three pallets, the furnishings of the house. The area below the house represents the road along which the SCHOLARS come. They enter from the left, cross below the house, stop and turn on the line: "Why there's a kind old man who appears . . ."

[*Playing time: 10 minutes.*]

FIRST SCHOLAR

Let us, who have come to this foreign land
In the search for further learning,

* The nature of this play may be too worldly for production in the church proper. The recreation room would perhaps be a better setting.

Seek a lodging close at hand
While yet the friendly sun is burning.

SECOND SCHOLAR

The sun holds back his horses on the shore,
But soon he'll plunge into the sea of night.
And since we've never seen this land before,
Your counsel seems most wise and right.
   (*The* OLD MAN *and his* WIFE *come out of the house as
if to enjoy the evening air.*)

THIRD SCHOLAR

Why, there's a kind old man who appears
Just at the time when we need him most.
Our prayers may fall on friendly ears,
And he may consent to be our host.
   (*They approach the* OLD MAN *and his* WIFE.)

FIRST SCHOLAR

Dear sir, we've come in search of learning
From our own land, a long and weary way.
Now night is falling. We are yearning
For sleep, and have no place to stay.

OLD MAN
(Curtly.)

Then call on the Lord's hospitality.
I'll give no bed or board to you;
This could not possibly benefit me.
I have better things to do.
   (*He turns away.*)

SECOND SCHOLAR
(*To the* OLD WOMAN.)

Perhaps, dear lady, you could find
Some way to help us in our need.
Though you'd gain nothing, you'd be kind,
And God would bless you for the deed.

OLD WOMAN
(*To her* HUSBAND.)

The ways of charity demand
We ask them in, as he requests.
These boys are in a foreign land.
Let's give them lodging as our guests.

OLD MAN

All right. If that's what you desire,
I will let them spend the night.
(*To the* SCHOLARS.)
Come in, then, scholars, to the fire.
We will help you in your plight.
(*The* SCHOLARS *enter the house. They lie down and
go to sleep.*)

OLD MAN
(*While the* SCHOLARS *sleep.*)

Their purses seem so fat to me;
There's no lack of money there.
If it weren't for the infamy,
We might do well—if we would dare.

OLD WOMAN

We've borne the yoke of poverty,
The wolf is always at the door.

If we should put to death these three,
We shouldn't be paupers anymore.

Therefore, now, unsheath your sword,
And kill these scholars, every one.
You shall be as rich as a lord;
No man will know what you have done.
> (*They murder the* SCHOLARS *and lay a cloth over them,
> to hide the bodies.*
>
> ST. NICHOLAS, *dressed as a wealthy traveler, enters
> right, and goes to the door of the house. He greets the*
> OLD MAN *and the* WOMAN.)

ST. NICHOLAS

I am a traveler, weary of the road.
It's night, and I would like to plead
For leave to rest in your abode.
It is useless to proceed.

OLD MAN
(*To the* OLD WOMAN.)

Shall I let him spend the night?
Dear wife, is that what you advise?

OLD WOMAN

His rank is such it seems but right.
To give him lodging would be wise.

OLD MAN

Traveler, since it is only meet
We show your rank respect, come in.
> (ST. NICHOLAS *enters the house.*)

St. Nicholas and the Scholars

And does your worship wish to eat?
> (ST. NICHOLAS *nods.*)

Then here is food for you.
> (*There is a pause.*)
> Begin.

ST. NICHOLAS

I cannot eat the food you offer.
There is a scent of evil in the air.

OLD MAN

It is the best we have to proffer
Your accusation's false, I swear.

ST. NICHOLAS

You lie to me! It's very plain.
I *know* there's evil in this house.
For hapless innocents are slain
By you and your rapacious spouse!

OLD MAN

Have mercy, sir, we beg of you!
We see you are a saint from heaven.

OLD WOMAN

Our crime is hateful, that is true,
But can our sin not be forgiven?

ST. NICHOLAS

Bring forth the bodies of the slain;
And be repentant for your crime!

By the grace of God may they live again,
And you win pardon in His good time.

>   (*The bodies are revealed to* ST. NICHOLAS.)

ST. NICHOLAS
(*Praying.*)

O, Holy God, O Father of men!
Maker of heaven, of earth and the sea!
Command these dead to live again,
And pardon these who cry to Thee!

>   (*The* SCHOLARS *come to life.* ST. NICHOLAS *disappears.*
>   *The* OLD MAN *and* WOMAN *are forgiven. The* CHOIR
>   *sings a hymn of praise.*)

PLAYS FOR

The Easter Season

The Fleury Sepulchre Play

CHARACTERS:

Mary Magdalene	*An Angel*
Second Mary	*Peter*
Third Mary	*John*

THE SCENE:

The scene represents the tomb of Christ, set in the chancel. The THREE MARYS enter from the transept left, and, as they approach the sepulchre, speak.
[*Playing time*: *10 minutes*.]

MARY MAGDALENE

Our holy Shepherd now is dead,
He who for all sinners bled.
   O wail, you people!

SECOND MARY

Our one true Shepherd now is gone,
Who brought the dead to life alone.
   O death of mourning!

THIRD MARY

Ah, what shall we do in our misery here,
Orphaned of our Master dear?
   O fortune of tears!

MARY MAGDALENE

Let us hasten on our way
To do what little yet we may
    With hearts devout!

SECOND MARY

With oils and spices, sweet and warm,
Let us anoint the sacred form,
    For it is precious!

THIRD MARY

What has the Prince of Justice done,
That they should crucify God's Son?
    O worship Him!

MARY MAGDALENE

But how shall we remove the stone,
We three women, weak and lone?
    O mourn with us!
    (*They reach the sepulchre and discover the* ANGEL,
    who stands beside it.)

ANGEL

Whom seek you in the sepulchre, O followers
    Of Christ?

ALL THREE MARYS

Jesus of Nazareth which was crucified,
    O Heavenly One.

ANGEL

Christians, why seek the living with the dead?
He is not here, but has arisen, as he said.

Remember how he spoke to you in Galilee,
That Christ must suffer death to set all sinners free,
And on the third day rise in His Divinity.
    (*The* ANGEL *disappears behind the sepulchre.*)

ALL THREE MARYS
    (*Leaving the sepulchre, they turn to the audience.*)

We came in sorrow to His tomb,
But He has overcome His doom
    And risen!
    (SECOND *and* THIRD MARY *leave as they entered.*)

MARY MAGDALENE
    (*Returning to the sepulchre, she looks within.*)

What sorrow! Ah, what aching pain!
I shall not see my Lord again!
    O who has stolen Him?
    (*She goes to the transept right where* PETER *and* JOHN
are standing.)
They have taken our Lord away
From the tomb in which He lay;
And there is nothing in it now,
But the cloth that bound His brow.
    (PETER *and* JOHN *run to the sepulchre.* JOHN *gets there
first, but remains outside,* PETER *enters the sepulchre,
followed by* JOHN. *They come out again immediately.*
MARY MAGDALENE *returns to the sepulchre, having fol-
lowed them slowly.*)

JOHN

How wonderful this thing we see!
    (*To* PETER, *incredulously.*)
Has He been stolen secretly?

PETER

No, I believe that, as He said,
He is risen from the dead.

JOHN

But why has He left within this place
The cloth that lay upon His face?

PETER

For linen now He has no need.
It is a sign He rose indeed.
> (PETER *and* JOHN *leave the sepulchre, and go out through the right transept door.* MARY MAGDALENE *remains by the sepulchre.*)

MARY MAGDALENE

What sorrow! Ah, what aching pain!
I shall not see my Lord again!
    O who has stolen Him?

ANGEL
> (*Returning to appear before the sepulchre.*)

Woman, why do you weep?

MARY MAGDALENE

They have taken our Lord away
From this tomb in which He lay,
    I know not where!

ANGEL

Weep not, Mary. The Lord is risen.
> (*He goes behind the sepulchre.*)

MARY MAGDALENE
(*Coming down to the crossing.*)

I seek my Lord! I'm sore dismayed!
I cannot find where He is laid!

JESUS
(*Dressed as a gardener, enters from the left transept
and meets her at the crossing.*)

Woman, why do you weep?
Whom do you seek?

MARY MAGDALENE

Tell me, sir, Oh, tell me, pray,
If you bore my Lord away!

JESUS

Mary!

MARY MAGDALENE
(*Falling at His feet.*)

Rabboni!

JESUS
(*Draws away from her.*)

Touch me not! For I am not yet ascended to my Father
and your Father, my God and your God! Fear not. Go and
tell my disciples to go into Galilee. There they will see me,
as I have foretold.
(JESUS *leaves as he entered.*)

MARY MAGDALENE
(*Turning to the audience.*)

Rejoice with me, all you
Who in the Lord delight!

For He whom I sought
   Appeared to me this night
And while I wept before the grave,
I saw my Lord, Who will us save!

> (*She goes out at transept right. The choir sings a triumphant hymn of the Resurrection in which the congregation joins.*)

The Journey to Emmaus

CHARACTERS:

First Pilgrim	*Ten Disciples*
Jesus	*The Choir*
Second Pilgrim	*Attendants*

THE SCENE:

In the chancel, which represents Emmaus, are set benches and a table. On the table are three shallow dishes, a loaf of uncut bread, and a chalice of wine. The transept represents the road to Emmaus. The CHOIR is in the choir stalls. TWO PILGRIMS enter the transept, left, singing an Easter hymn. As they finish they pantomime conversation, seeming troubled. JESUS enters the transept right, dressed as a pilgrim, and meets them at the crossing.
[*Playing time: 10 minutes.*]

JESUS

What manner of communications are these that you have one to another as you walk and are sad?

FIRST PILGRIM

Are you only a stranger in Jerusalem, and do you not know the things which have come to pass there in these days?

JESUS

What things?

SECOND PILGRIM

Concerning Jesus of Nazareth, Who was a prophet, mighty in deed and in word before God and all the people.

FIRST PILGRIM

How the chief priests and our rulers delivered Him to be condemned to death and have crucified Him.

SECOND PILGRIM

And today is the third day since these things were done.

JESUS
(*As if rebuking them.*)

O fools and slow of heart to believe all that the prophets have spoken! Ought not Christ to have suffered these things and to enter His glory?
(*He starts to leave, but the* PILGRIMS *detain Him.*)

FIRST PILGRIM

Abide with us, for it is towards evening, and the day is far spent.

SECOND PILGRIM

Your words please us, that you speak concerning the resurrection of our Master.
(*All three go to the place, set in the chancel, which represents Emmaus, and sit at the table. Attendants bring them water that they may wash their hands.*

JESUS *takes the bread, and, raising His right hand, gives the blessing. Then He breaks the bread into separate portions, saying:*)

JESUS

Peace I leave with you; my peace I give you.
(*Passing the chalice to the* FIRST PILGRIM, *He rises, goes to the chancel steps, and speaks:*)
These are the words which I spoke to you while I was yet with you. Even as my Father has loved me, so I have loved you; do you continue in my love.
(*He goes out as He came in. The* PILGRIMS *rise, startled, and, as they come down to the crossing looking after Him, call out in loud voices.*)

FIRST PILGRIM

Did not our hearts burn within us for Jesus while He talked with us by the way?

SECOND PILGRIM

And while He opened the Scriptures to us?

FIRST PILGRIM

Alas, where were our wretched senses?

SECOND PILGRIM

Where had our minds gone?
(*The* PILGRIMS *run to the* CHOIR, *ten of whom are together, representing the* DISCIPLES *without* THOMAS.)

THE PILGRIMS

The Lord is risen!

THE TEN

The Lord is risen, indeed, and has appeared to Peter!
(*The* PILGRIMS *take their places with the* DISCIPLES.)

JESUS
(*Re-enters by the chancel door.*)

Peace be with you. I live. Fear not.

CHOIR
(*In terror.*)

Who is this that comes from Edom, with dyed garments
from Bosrah?

JESUS

Peace be with you.

CHOIR
(*Still terrified.*)

Who is glorious in His apparel, traveling in the great-
ness of His strength?

JESUS

Why are you troubled, and why do thoughts arise in
your hearts? Behold my hands and my feet, that it is I,
myself.
(*He shows them His reddened hands and feet. The*
DISCIPLES *are still hesitant.*)
Touch me and see; for a spirit has not flesh and bones
as you see I have. Now believe.
(*They come to Him in the chancel, and touch His
hands and feet. They kneel before Him. He raises
His hand over them.*)

Receive the Holy Ghost. Whose soever sins you remit, they are remitted unto them.

(He leaves again as He came.)

THE CHOIR
(As THOMAS *enters from the left transept.)*

The Lord is risen from the tomb,
Who hung for us upon the tree.
Alleluia, alleluia, alleluia!

*(*THOMAS *reaches the group.)*

Thomas, we have seen the Lord!

THOMAS

Except I shall see in His hands the print of the nails, and thrust my hand into His side, I will not believe.

JESUS
(Returning by the chancel door, comes down to meet THOMAS *on the chancel steps.)*

Peace be with you.

CHOIR

This is the Lord's doing, and it is marvellous in our eyes. This is the day which the Lord has made; let us rejoice and be glad in it.

JESUS
(Holding out his hands.)

Thomas, behold my wounds.

(Taking THOMAS' *hand.)*

Reach hither your hand and tell the places where the nails were put, and be not faithless, but believing.

THOMAS

(Having touched the wounds, falls at JESUS' *feet.)*

My Lord and my God.

JESUS

Thomas, because you have seen me, you have believed.
Blessed are they that have not seen, and yet have believed.
(The DISCIPLES *lead* JESUS *out, by the left transept
door, singing a triumphant hymn of the Resurrection. The congregation joins in the singing.)*

The King of Glory

CHARACTERS:

Narrator   An Angel
Pilate   The Three Marys
Caiaphas   Peter and John
Annas   Jesus
Three Soldiers The Choir

THE SCENE:

Three places are represented in this scene. The tomb
of Christ is in the chancel, PILATE's throne room is in
the transept right. The main doors of the church
will be used to represent the gates of Hell. The CHOIR
is divided into two sections, one of which is in the
choir stalls, the other in the vestry. At the beginning
of the play, the NARRATOR enters from the chancel
and goes to the pulpit, or reading stand.
[Playing time: 20 minutes.]

NARRATOR

Pilate entered with Jesus into the Praetorium, and he said
to Him: "You are the King of the Jews?" And Jesus answered, "You say that I am the King." Then Jesus went
out of the Praetorium, and the soldiers dressed Him in
purple vestments and a crown of thorns; and when they had
been put upon Him, the crowd cried: "Let Him be cruci-

fied, because He has made Himself the Son of God!" And
Pilate said to them: "Is it your will that I shall crucify your
King?" And the High Priests answered: "We have no
King, save only Caesar!"

(*The* NARRATOR *goes out as he came.* PILATE *enters
and sits in a high seat in the transept right. He is
followed by* CAIAPHAS, ANNAS, *and* THREE SOLDIERS.)

CAIAPHAS

Lord Governor, we remember well
What we have heard from common men,
That their Seducer used to tell:
"In three days I shall rise again."

PILATE

Caiaphas, I can plainly see—
But let me tell you it's in vain—
You seek to lay the blame on me
For Jesus' death, that He is slain.

ANNAS
(*Ignoring* PILATE's *statement.*)

Therefore now your soldiers tell—
Lest His disciples come by night
And rob the grave—to watch it well;
Or men will think He told them right.

PILATE

Go, stand guard the tomb about,
And keep His body safe imprisoned,
Lest these others steal Him out
And people think their King is risen.

CAIAPHAS
(Paying the SOLDIERS *gold.)*

We need, good sirs, your honor bright,
Your courage and your swords, your name
As soldiers; for His followers might
Make ruin of our people's fame.

FIRST SOLDIER
(To CAIAPHAS.*)*

Thank you, Priest, for this reward!

SECOND SOLDIER
(Brandishing his weapon.)

You may depend upon this sword!

THIRD SOLDIER
(To PILATE.*)*

We shall maintain your honor, lord.
(The SOLDIERS *proceed to the tomb in the chancel.*
PILATE *and the* PRIESTS *go out by the near transept*
door.)

FIRST SOLDIER
(At the tomb.)

Christ will never rise today,
But lest they steal this corpse away
We watch our nightly vigils well:
On guard! For horrors who can tell!

SECOND SOLDIER

The human mind does not allow
That the dead shall rise; yet now,

Seducers plot their tricks too well:
On guard! For horrors who can tell!

THIRD SOLDIER

If that the dead can rise again,
Who might have stayed alive, why then
Bore He the pains of death and hell?
On guard! For horrors who can tell!

ANGEL

(*Enters silently from the chancel door, carrying an unsheathed sword.*)

The Shepherd now His sheep will save,
For He has risen from the grave!

(*He touches one of the soldiers with his sword and the three fall to the ground. The* ANGEL *stands by the tomb.*)

Man on this morning wakes to find
Christ pleads the cause of humankind.
His sacrifice of blood is done,
He has a greater glory won.
No longer does the Father's power
Walk the earth as flesh and bone,
But in this glorious morning hour
He makes His blessedness your own.
Blessed be the Father and the Son;
Blessed be the conquest He has won!

(*During this and the following brief scene, the* SOLDIERS *remain lying on the ground as if stunned. The* THREE MARYS *enter from the transept left.*)

FIRST MARY

We seek for a price, some precious spice,
    Unguent of Orient breath.

SECOND MARY

Sweet-scented be His pyre to me,
  In memory of His death.

SPICE MERCHANT

(Following them in, catches up with them at the crossing.)

Fair are the ointments fresh I bring,
Our Savior's bleeding wounds to lave,
In glory of His name, our King,
In memory of His holy grave.

  (The THREE MARYS *in brief pantomime buy spices from the* MERCHANT *and pay for them. He leaves as he came. The* MARYS *proceed to the tomb.)*

THIRD MARY

Who will roll away the stone
From the doorway to His tomb?

ANGEL

(Still standing by the entrance to the tomb.)

Why do you seek the living with the dead?
He is not here, as you may see.
He is arisen, as He said
Before this death, in Galilee.
You seek Jesus.
      (The MARYS *fall back from the tomb.)*
            Have no fear.
He is arisen. He is not here.
      (Pointing into the tomb.)
See here the spot He lay upon.
Go, tell His disciples He has gone

Before you into Galilee.
There your meeting place shall be.
> (*The* ANGEL *leaves as he came. The* THREE MARYS *go out by the transept doors, left. The* SOLDIERS *awaken, pantomime their shock at the discovery that the tomb is empty, and hurry to* PILATE *and the* PRIESTS *who have resumed their places during the* SOLDIERS' *pantomime.*)

FIRST SOLDIER

As we were standing guard there, sir,
Remaining steadfast at our posts,
There came a dark-winged messenger,
Who told us that the Lord of Hosts
Had risen.

SECOND SOLDIER

And then beside the sepulchre
We saw a throng of dreadful ghosts,
The whole earth quaked, we felt it stir,
And saw the martyred Lord of Hosts
Depart His prison.

CAIAPHAS
> (*Giving the* SOLDIERS *money.*)

Here, take this money as your fee.
We want this old-wives' tale suppressed.
As for this rumor—let it be.
The people must not be distressed.

ANNAS

And when you are abroad, take care,
And say the body was taken away.

Tell them: "At night a thief came there,
And stole Him from the place He lay."
> (*Nodding and smiling among themselves,* PILATE,
> ANNAS *and* CAIAPHAS *go out the same way they en-
> tered.*)
> (*The* SOLDIERS *advance toward the congregation and
> say, in a confidential tone:*)

FIRST SOLDIER

We wearied in the darkening gloom,
And lay upon the ground and slept.

SECOND SOLDIER

Some thieves came running to the tomb,
And took their Master out, and wept.
> (*They follow the others out. The* THREE MARYS, PETER
> *and* JOHN *enter the transept, left.*)

SECOND MARY

We can see the angel's face, and hear
His answer still, that rang out clear!
It witnesses our Lord *does* live,
So Peter, now you *must* believe.

PETER

This seems a madman's dream to me!
Who would believe such things could be?
> (PETER *and* JOHN *run to the tomb, as the* FIRST *and*
> SECOND MARY *leave.* JOHN *reaches the tomb first and
> finds the napkin.*)

JOHN

The tomb is empty, still and cold;
Not here His wounded body lies.

Can it be as He foretold?
Can the dead to life arise?

PETER

(*Holding up the linen winding bands for the congregation to see.*)

The tomb is empty, cold and still;
His wounded body lies not here.
Could He arise from death at will?
Or has some thief defiled the bier?

(*They go out, pantomiming conversation, the way
they came in.*)

MARY MAGDALENE

(*Who has followed them to the sepulchre.*)

Lo, the stone is rolled away
That sealed His tomb, my Master dear!
Soldiers watched by night and day,
But it is empty. He is not here!

How can my heart this grief contain
For my Holy Master's leaving?
He hailed me fair, though full of pain,
Drove out my sins, but left me grieving.

JESUS

(*Coming in by the chancel door, in the guise of a
gardener, followed by the* ANGEL.)

Woman, why do you weep?

MARY

They have taken away my Lord,
And I know not where they have laid Him.

JESUS

Woman, why do you weep?
Whom do you seek?

MARY

If you have taken Him away,
Tell me where you have laid Him,
And I shall take Him up.

JESUS

Mary!

MARY

Rabboni!

JESUS
(As MARY *bends to touch His feet.)*

Do not touch me, for I am not yet ascended to my Father,
but go to my brethren and tell them: I shall arise to my
Father and your Father, my God and your God.

(MARY *assents mutely, and goes out by the transept
door, left, her face transfigured. The* ANGEL *precedes*
JESUS *down through the aisle of the church toward
the front door which represents the gates of Hell.
A portion of the* CHOIR *is stationed in the vestry, to
represent the people of Hell.)*

THE ANGEL *
(As they advance down the aisle, singing:)

When Christ, the King of Glory,
Would storm the gates of Hell,

* For music to *The King of Glory* and *Thou Art Here,* see pp. 274
and 275.

Before His face the angel choirs
Majestic numbers tell.

The thousands of the blessed,
Who captive lie in death,
With sobbing and with sighing,
Answer that holy breath!
    (*A wordless, harmonic wail is heard from the* PEOPLE
    beyond the gate.)

JESUS
(*Before the doors, loudly.*)

Lift up your gates, O, you Princes of Darkness!
And be you lifted up, you everlasting doors!
And the King of Glory shall come in!

A BASS VOICE
(*From within.*)

Who is this King of Glory?

JESUS

He is the Lord, strong and mighty!
Even the Lord, mighty in battle!
    (JESUS *pushes open the doors. The* PEOPLE *sing*:)

CHOIR *

Thou art here, Desire of Nations;
In darkness long we've lain!
Lead us out, O Lord, this night
From prison and from pain!

Thee we've called upon with sighing,
In time of trouble, Thee!

   * For music to *The King of Glory* and *Thou Art Here*, see pp. 274
and 275.

Thou art the hope of the hopeless, Thou,
A rock in misery!

> (*The doors close. The remainder of the* CHOIR *in the*
> *stalls begins a triumphant hymn of the Resurrection,*
> *in which the congregation joins.*)

The Resurrection of Christ

CHARACTERS:

Pilate	Centurio
Caiaphas	Jesus
Annas	The Three Marys
Soldiers	Two Angels

The Choir

THE SCENE:

Two places are represented in the scene. The tomb of Christ is in the chancel. In the transept right is the throne room of PILATE. Present are PILATE, seated on his throne, CAIAPHAS, ANNAS, and some SOLDIERS. The CHOIR is in the choir stalls.

[*Playing time*: *25 minutes*.]

PILATE

(*Rising from his seat, addresses the congregation.*)

You should know that I am Pilate,
Who, in solemn judgment, sat
At Calvary of late.
Yes, this very morn,
I, the ruler of the state,
Hanged a man they crowned with thorns.

(He returns to his seat, addresses CAIAPHAS.)

Since that rebel now is dead,
Caiaphas, let this word be spread,
"Search the land, and if you find
Others with His creed,
Or any leaders of His kind,
Remind them of this morning's deed."

CAIAPHAS

Sir, I think we need not fear,
I see Centurio coming here,
The knight we left to guard the cross,
Lest Jesus' followers rebel.
He would not leave and come to us,
Except if all were well.
  (CENTURIO, *having entered the transept left, reaches
the group.)*

CENTURIO

God save you, sirs, on every side!
May health and wealth with you abide!

PILATE

Centurio! Welcome to this place,
Our faithful knight!

CENTURIO

I thank you, sir. God grant you grace,
And rule you right.

PILATE

Centurio, draw near at hand,
And tell me tidings of my land.

For you have known my people long,
And known them well.

CENTURIO

Great sir, I fear you have done wrong,
The truth to tell.

CAIAPHAS

Done wrong? I pray you, how?
Explain it to us, here and now!

CENTURIO

So shall I, sir, if I'm not stilled,
As best I can.
The righteous Man Whom you have killed
Was more than man.

PILATE

Centurio, you have no right
To speak like this, you faithless knight!
If we should need your help some day
To bear us out.
It would be traitorous, I say,
Our will to flout.

CENTURIO

To bear out *truth* is good, say I,
But when I saw this Jesus die,
I knew it was God's Son
Whom we had slain!
I say it now to everyone,
And so I will maintain.

ANNAS

Centurio, you'll live to rue
A statement that we know untrue—
Unless you bring some proof that sunders
All our doubt.

CENTURIO

The world has never seen such wonders
As came about.

The sun in woe waxed pale and wan;
The shining moon and stars were gone.
The whole earth trembled as the Man
Looked down and spoke.
The stones that never stir, began
To shudder, burst and broke!

And dead men rose up from the grave.

PILATE

Centurio, cease, you foolish knave!
You know the scholars give a reason
For such a sight.
"Eclipse," they say, when for a season
Sun and moon give forth no light.

CAIAPHAS

If dead men rise up bodily,
That may be done by sorcery.
And therefore we cannot set store
By what you say.

CENTURIO

I will believe forevermore
What I have seen this day.

It's not the evil work you've done,
Nor just the darkening of the sun,
But why the covenant split in two,
That's what I wonder!

PILATE

Such tales if told by you,
Would split the land asunder!

Traitor! Do you dare before our eyes
Try to catch us with such lies?
Get out! I hope to see you hang,
You lying thief!

CAIAPHAS

You'll learn to cease your false harangue,
Or come to grief!

CENTURIO

Since you'll not hear the truth from me,
I bid you, sirs, good day.
God grant that you'll be made to see
The truth some other way.

ANNAS

Since you're afraid, get out of here!
What we have done, we do not fear!
                    (CENTURIO *goes out right.*)

PILATE

Such wonderful things as Centurio told
Never were before.
To settle this we must be bold;
We shall hear more!

For Jesus when he came to die,
Said to the men who passed Him by—
A thing that threatens you and me,
As well it may—
That He would rise up bodily,
The third day.

If it is really as He said,
The latter thing is more to dread,
Than was the first. We must take heed,
And plan our course.
Be on your guard, for you shall need
More guile than force.

ANNAS

Sir, even if He did say so,
He has no might to rise and go.
But they might steal His corpse away
And hide it well.
And that would be a bitter day,
The truth to tell.

It would be said by everyone
That He had risen all alone.
Therefore send men to guard that stone
And keep it fast,

Till these three days have come and gone,
And all is past.

PILATE

Good Annas, what you say is true;
The thing that you advise, I'll do.
I'll send the guard this very day,
And He'll not rise,
Nor shall they dare steal Him away
From where He lies.

(*He addresses the* SOLDIERS.)

Soldiers, go guard by day and night
The body of Jesus with all your might!
Keep Him safe these next three days
Within His tomb.
If you do this, you'll win my praise,
If not, you seal your doom.

FIRST SOLDIER

Yes, Sir Pilate, we obey,
Where He lies, there shall He stay.
Nor any traitor in this land
Shall take Him from that spot.

SECOND SOLDIER

Our arms are ready here at hand.
We linger not.

(*They cross to the sepulchre which is set in the chancel.* PILATE *and his retinue go out right.*)

On every side we'll guard the cave
With steel-clad might.

Whoever comes to rob the grave,
We'll kill on sight.

FIRST SOLDIER

Who'll sit where, I want to know?

SECOND SOLDIER

This is the place where I will go.

THIRD SOLDIER

And I shall go sit at His feet.

FOURTH SOLDIER

And I go here.
Now, by the gods, I'd like to meet
Who dares appear.
    (*Music. The* SOLDIERS *fall asleep.* CHRIST *rises from the tomb.*)

JESUS
(*To the congregation.*)

Earthly man that I have wrought,
Wake at once and sleep you nought!
With bitter bail I have you bought,
To make you free.
Into this dungeon deep I sought,
And all for love of thee.

Behold how dear the price I give,
The bloody wounds—that you may live.
Full dear I bought you, sinful man,
And suffered keen;

Do not defile yourself again,
Now you are clean.

(JESUS *retires behind the sepulchre, and the* THREE MARYS *advance from the transept left.*)

MARY MAGDALENE

Alas, alas, I die of grief!
This sorrow passes all belief.
There is no glimmer in this night
That I can see.
My Lord, Who was the source of light
Is dead from me.

MARY JACOBY

Alas, how can I stand the pain,
When I think that He is slain?
He died unto Himself alone,
As He foresaid.

MARY SALOME

Who now shall listen to my moan?
My Lord is dead!

MARY MAGDALENE

Since He is dead, my sisters dear,
No use in our lamenting here.
Let's take our oils to where He's laid,
And lies asleep,
To dress the wounds the wicked made,
His wounds so deep.

MARY JACOBY

Let's go then, sisters, to that place.
I long to look upon His face.

But even so, I cannot see,
Since we're alone,
How three weak women, such as we,
Can move that stone.

MARY SALOME

No, that we surely cannot do,
For it is huge, and heavy, too.

MARY MAGDALENE

It will be moved though, sisters, when
We reach the cave.
For there I see two white-clothed men
Beside the grave.

MARY JACOBY

And now I see it's as you say,
The heavy stone is moved away.

MARY SALOME

I wonder, now, what that may mean,
So let us go,
And ask the men if they have seen,
The One we worship so.
          (*They approach the sepulchre.*)

FIRST ANGEL
(*In the forefront of the* CHOIR)

You mourning women, mild and meek,
Whom is it you have come to seek?

MARY MAGDALENE

Jesus, Who was cruelly slain,
Our Lord so dear.

SECOND ANGEL
(Beside the FIRST.)

O women, you have come in vain;
He is not here.

FIRST ANGEL

No, He is gone, the truth to say.
The place is empty where He lay.
He will be found in Galilee.
Now go and tell
All those who mourn this villainy
That all is well.

MARY JACOBY

As we have heard, so shall we say,
Mary Magdalene, good day.

MARY MAGDALENE

Farewell.
    (They go as they came. MARY MAGDALENE *remains.)*
        Oh, think of that sweet blood,
How it was spilt!
Though He was never aught but good,
And knew no guilt.

It was for me He suffered pain!
It was my guilt that He was slain!
Oh, I should fall and kiss His feet
If He were here.
There's nothing now, until we meet,
Will give me cheer.
    (She stands aside, weeping. The SOLDIERS *wake, one
    after the other.)*

FIRST SOLDIER

Ah, alas, what shall I say?
The body is not where it lay!

SECOND SOLDIER

He's gone? Alas, we've come to grief;
He is not here?

FIRST SOLDIER

Get up and see!

SECOND SOLDIER

The scoundrel! Thief!

FIRST SOLDIER

We shall pay dear!

THIRD SOLDIER
(*Waking.*)

What devil ails you two?
Why do you make this great to-do?

SECOND SOLDIER

Because He's gone! That's why we shout.

FOURTH SOLDIER
(*Waking.*)

What do you say?

SECOND SOLDIER

Someone has come and stolen Him out.

FOURTH SOLDIER

They've taken Him away?

FIRST SOLDIER

Alas, what shall we do, we four,
Since this body's here no more?
I think, my friends, we'd better swear
He rose alone.

SECOND SOLDIER

When Pilate hears of this affair,
He'll make us groan.

FIRST SOLDIER

He rose all by Himself, I know.

SECOND SOLDIER

Why, I myself—I saw Him go!

THIRD SOLDIER

He couldn't rise if He were dead;
You know that's so.

FOURTH SOLDIER
(*Stupidly.*)

I slept upon this rocky bed;
I couldn't know.

FIRST SOLDIER
(*Patiently.*)

If Pilate hears about this theft,
That we were sleeping when He left,

There is no question but we'll be
In great disgrace.

FOURTH SOLDIER
(Nodding.)

Yes, we must lie, that's plain to see,
To save our face.

THIRD SOLDIER

What you say is very true.

SECOND SOLDIER

And I am in agreement, too.

THIRD SOLDIER

A thousand carried Him away
At dark midnight.
And we were nearly slain, I'll say,
Such was the fight.

FOURTH SOLDIER

No sirs, I hold no lie so good,
As simple truth, just as it stood.
I think He simply rose up so,
And went His way.
And if Sir Pilate wants to know,
That's what I'll say.

FIRST SOLDIER

Why, soldier, do you dare to go
To Pilate's court and tell him so?
(The FOURTH SOLDIER *nods.)*

SECOND SOLDIER

(*After a pause, steps forward.*)

I, too, am of the same belief.
We die but once.

THIRD SOLDIER

And He who brought us all this grief,
Woe to His bones!
   (*They go to* PILATE, *who has entered with* CAIAPHAS
   and ANNAS, *right.*)

FIRST SOLDIER

Sir Pilate, prince without a peer!

PILATE

Most mighty knights, you're welcome here!
But tell us everything about
What you have wrought.

FIRST SOLDIER

Our watching, Lord, without a doubt
Has come to nought.

CAIAPHAS

(*Horrified.*)

To nought? Alas, don't tell us so.

SECOND SOLDIER

The prophet, Jesus, whom you know,
Has risen living from the dead,
In all His might!

The Resurrection of Christ 153

PILATE

The devil's curses on your head,
Vile, traitorous knight!

Why, you cowards, dare you say
That you have let him get away?

THIRD SOLDIER

Sir, no man dared draw a breath
When He appeared.

FOURTH SOLDIER

We all fell down as if in death,
And shook with fear.

FIRST SOLDIER

We were so frightened, everyone,
When Jesus put aside the stone.
We shook with fear and dared not stir,
Nor speak a word.

PILATE

But was He all alone there, sir?

SECOND SOLDIER

Yes, lord, as you have heard.

PILATE

We are destroyed by treachery!
Our laws are made a mockery!
Caiaphas! Caiaphas, tell me now,
What shall we do?

CAIAPHAS
(*Muttering.*)

If I knew aught, why sir, I vow,
I'd tell you true!

ANNAS
(*Whispers.*)

This is the best advice I know;
It would be wise to manage so
That these four knights take back their story.
It will not do.
For it would bring us endless worry,
If anyone knew.

And for this end, my worthy lord,
You might give each a good reward.

PILATE

This counsel serves our purpose well.
It shall be thus.
(*Aloud to the knights.*)
Defenders of our citadel,
Attend to us:

Listen to me, my soldiers brave,
You must say this about the grave:
Ten thousand well-armed men
Came there last night,
And took away His corpse again
In bitter fight.

And here is gold as your reward.

FIRST SOLDIER

FIRST SOLDIER

You may depend on us, my lord;
In every country, no matter where
We chance to stray,
We shall tell the story there,
Just as you say.

>   (PILATE *leads his retinue off, right. At the sepulchre,*
>   JESUS, *in the guise of a gardener, appears from behind
>   the tomb.* MARY MAGDALENE *advances to him.*)

MARY MAGDALENE

Tell me, gardener, I pray,
If you bore my Lord away?
Tell me where he is.

>   (JESUS *makes a motion as if to leave.*)
>   Oh, stay,

And tell me, man.
I shall remove Him if I may,
And if I can.

JESUS

Woman, why do you weep? Be still.
Whom do you seek? Tell me your will.

MARY

I am looking for My Lord,
Where He is laid.
If I find Him I have adored,
I am well paid.

JESUS

Woman, woman, turn your thought.
You knew well I hid Him not.

Nor took Him anywhere with me.
                    (*Pointing to the sepulchre.*)
Have you looked within this ground?

MARY

Ah, yes. In faith, I cannot see
Where He'll be found.

JESUS

Why woman, what was He to you,
That you should grieve?

MARY

To me He was a new . . .
                    (*She breaks off.*)
I can no longer live.

JESUS

It is your God you wish to see —
And I am He!

    (MARY MAGDALENE *recognizes Him and falls at His feet.*)

MARY

Rabboni! Oh, my Lord so dear!
Now I am well, since You are here!
Suffer me to touch Your hand
And kiss Your feet!
I would obey your least command,
My Lord, as is but meet!

JESUS
(Drawing back.)

Ask no more but that we met.
I have not ascended yet.
Tell my brethren I shall be
Before them all in Trinity,
Whose Will in this I've wrought.
Their peace has now been bought,
Who deep in sin did pine,
And so be grateful in your thought
To God, your Lord and mine.

Mary, you must quickly go
To my disciples, tell them so.
They are amazed and wrapped in woe.
Say that they shall grieve no more
In any way for me;
For I, myself, shall go before
Them all to Galilee.

MARY

Lord, I shall carry out the task,
And make them happy, as You ask.
                    (JESUS *leaves by the chancel door.*)
My bliss has come! My care is gone,
Since I have met that lovely One.
I know a joy I never knew
By day or night.
Now He is risen, Whom they slew,
My heart is light!

I am as light as leaf on tree,
For well I know that it was He,

The joyfullest sight that one could see,
My Lord Jesu!
And he who did that treachery,
Long may he rue!

To His disciples I will fare
In Galilee, and ease their care.
I know that they will mourn no more
When they hear this.

            (To the congregation.)

And may that Child that Mary bore
Bring you to bliss!

    (She goes out by the transept doors, left, as the CHOIR
    begins a hymn of the Resurrection.)

The Redentin Easter Play*

CHARACTERS:

Two Angels

Caiaphas

Two Priests

Pilate

Four Soldiers

Watchman

Jesus

Annas

Servant

A Bass Voice

The Choir

THE SCENE:

Three places are represented. In the transept left is the synagogue. In the transept right, PILATE's throne room. The tomb of CHRIST is set in the chancel. The CHOIR is in the choir stalls. At the beginning of the play, all three scenes are bare. The ANGELS enter from the chancel, come down to the chancel steps and speak to the congregation.

[*Playing time*: 25 *minutes*.]

FIRST ANGEL

Be silent all alike,
Both poor and rich!
We shall give you a picture
Of how there arose from the dead

* Reprinted from *Redentin Easter Play*, translated by A. E. Zucker. Copyright 1941 by Columbia University Press.

God's Son, Jesus Christ,
Who died for you.
How the resurrection took place
That you would all like to see.

SECOND ANGEL

Sit down and rejoice,
Those who are now assembled here!
Rejoice! In this day
You may be freed of your sins:
God will at this time redeem those
Who leave off from evil;
Those who arise with God today,
They shall go free of sin.
That this may happen to all of you,
Let each hear and see!

(*The* ANGELS *go out as they came.*)

FIRST PRIEST

(*To* CAIAPHAS, ANNAS *and several other* PRIESTS *in the synagogue, transept left.*)

Caiaphas and all you assembled lords,
I shall tell you something.
This Jesus pretended to be God's son;
He said that He would overcome death.
He spoke such gruesome words
As never were heard from any man:
He would rise on the third day.
Therefore I say this to you:
You must have His grave guarded,
So that He cannot escape us.
If His disciples secretly snatch Him away,
Then they will say He rose from the dead.

CAIAPHAS

Ah, you are speaking the truth
If it should happen that His disciples
Should steal Him and take Him away,
We would be very much put to shame.
If you act on my advice,
Then you should quickly make ready
And go to Pilate,
And make him understand this argument
Just as you yourself have heard it.

FIRST PRIEST

That we will do immediately.
    (*The* PRIESTS *leave* CAIAPHAS *and* ANNAS *and cross to*
    PILATE *in the transept right.*)

FIRST PRIEST
(*To* PILATE.)

God greet you, Lord Pilate!

PILATE

Speak up, priest! What news do you bring?

SECOND PRIEST

Pilate, we ask that you shall in kindness receive
The story that we tell to you.
Pilate, we need your aid.
We beg you by the living God
Who created leaves and grass
That you have Jesus who appeared before your court
Most carefully guarded.
We fear lest His disciples come

And take away His corpse,
And then tell loudly everywhere
That Jesus has arisen.
Then we should have to shrink in deep disgrace.

PILATE

Nonsense! Are you beginning to rave?
Do you believe that a dead man can come to life?
Leave off this talk
And guard the grave yourselves!

FIRST PRIEST

Pilate, won't you please consider;
I have not forgotten it:
Jesus often gave His disciples to understand
That on the third day He would go forth from the grave
    alive.
This He said quite openly.
Therefore we fear His host of followers—
For there are untold numbers of them—
Lest someone should steal the corpse.
So send us a guard,
Most kind Pilate!

PILATE

If I want to live in peace,
Then I must send you guards and watchmen.
                    (*To his* SOLDIERS.)
My proud knights,
You will get silver and gold
For guarding Jesus,
Whom they call the Nazarene.

Watch well about the grave,
So that no one makes off with the corpse.

FIRST SOLDIER

Now look here, for what reason
Are we to watch a dead person?
You are afraid where there is nothing to fear.

SECOND SOLDIER

What harm could that do us?
We will take their money
And with it go to the grave.
If they will give us that reward,
We will as lief guard a dead man as a living one.

FIRST SOLDIER

Faith, then I shall be one of the guards.
If I am there He shall not rise!

SECOND SOLDIER

I will be the second watchman,
Though it cost me my life.
Such a disgrace will never happen to us
As that He should arise from the dead.
I will say it even now!

THIRD SOLDIER

I like this speech very well.
I want to be your companion, too,
And help you guard Him so well
That He shall not escape from us.
Be He ever so nimble,
We will hold Him to the end.

FOURTH SOLDIER

I, too, am a strong hero;
I, too, shall help you hold this field.
With faithfulness and honor
Shall I serve Pilate my lord.

FIRST PRIEST

Knights, you will never rue this.
I shall tell you in good faith:
If you guard that Hero well,
You will get ready cash
Paid up on the counter.

FIRST SOLDIER

Now step forward, you fighters,
Let's march to the grave;
Money makes the hero jump,
Well then, I'll lead the tune.

(PILATE *leads his* SOLDIERS *to the sepulchre in the chancel.*)

PILATE

Solomon, you're the best, I think;
You shall lie here in the west
If you let Him steal away,
You shall be banished from this land!

FIRST SOLDIER

I'm going to lie in the west,
For I am the best, I think.
I shall guard this place;
If anyone passes here,

I shall meet him in such a way
That he'd rather he were dead already.

PILATE

Samson, you shall be here in the north
And thus fulfill my command,
If you want to receive the reward from me.
I am your friend without any deception.
Be faithful and true in my service;
I will pay you a rich reward.
And consider this above all:
A good deed is never wasted.

SECOND SOLDIER

I'll lie here in the north.
If anyone comes here, I'll murder him
Be he tame or wild!

PILATE

Hear, my good man Boas von Thamar!
You're pretty clumsy when it comes to thinking;
Now try to be a bit nimble
And follow my instructions.
You shall stretch out in the east,
And if someone should try to carry off Jesus
See to it!
He must never do us any harm again.

THIRD SOLDIER

I'll lie down in the east
And rely on my bright sword.
I'll pick this very spot;
My honor shall not suffer the least stain.

PILATE

My faithful knight Sadoch
Up to the present you've always proved capable.
I shall place you in the south;
You shall prove your valor
By keeping watch on this occasion,
For it is not without danger.
If He should arise in the third night,
We should all suffer disgrace!

FOURTH SOLDIER

I shall lie here on the south side.
He is not going to walk or ride away from us.
So all of you help me keep watch
And don't be tricked by sleep.
He'll not escape from us.
> (PILATE *leaves them, and goes out by the right transept
> doors. The* WATCHMAN *comes in from the chancel
> door.*)

WATCHMAN

You knights and you heroes,
Think of the money
Which has been promised you!
Each one of you act the part of a man.
If this thing should happen,
I'll help you with my music.

FIRST SOLDIER

Watchman, my dear friend,
Wake with us in this hour.
Be faithful and kind to us;

That will get you gold and silver.
>   (*He lies down to sleep.*)

WATCHMAN

Wake, bold knight!
Between Hiddensee and Mone
There I see two;
They are floating in the wild sea
In a boat, as it seems to me.
Now, bold knight, take care!

SECOND SOLDIER

Watchman, my dear fellow,
Tell me, when they reach us.
Then I'll get ready to defend myself
And will speak to my companions.
>   (*He lies down to sleep.*)

WATCHMAN

Wake, proud knight
And earn your gold with honor!
Wake, knight, it is the hour of midnight!
I hear the dogs barking loud.
They howl and bark.
Talk to your companions!

THIRD SOLDIER

My dear brother Watchman,
I'll give you all my treasure
If I may only sleep a little bit.
>   (*He lies down to sleep.*)

FOURTH SOLDIER

I must give some rest to my eyes,
Even though I be exiled because of it.
                    (*He too, sleeps.*)
        (*The* WATCHMAN *looks at the sleeping* SOLDIERS,
        shrugs his shoulders, lies down and falls asleep. The
        TWO ANGELS *re-enter by the chancel door.*)

FIRST ANGEL

Sleep ye watchmen by the grave!
Since God has work in hand
Do no attempt to hinder it.

SECOND ANGEL

Awake! Why sleepest Thou, O Lord?
Arise, cast us not off forever!

FIRST ANGEL

Arise, O Son of God,
Whose subjects we, too, are!
Arise, Divine Consolation!
All guilt is now redeemed;
Everything will now be perfect,
Since You have added to Your human form
The divine glory
Which now You show forth bodily.

SECOND ANGEL

Arise, Lord, from Your sleep,
To the joy of all mankind!
Arise, O Man of God!
Thou shalt suffer no more pain or anguish.

Arise from all Thy sufferings!
Thou art an everlasting light!

JESUS
(*Appearing from the tomb.*)

I have risen and am still with thee!
(*He comes forward.*)
Now all things are accomplished
Which had been conceived of in eternity:
That I should die a bitter death
And gain salvation for mankind.
(*To the* ANGELS.)
Come now, let us prepare
To rescue those who sit in Hell.
(*He and the* ANGELS *go out the chancel door.*)

WATCHMAN
(*Waking.*)

Awake, knights, it's almost day!
I hear the song of the morning star.
(*He blows his horn three times.*)
There is dew in the fields.
Proud knight, break your rest.
(*He blows again more loudly.*)
Help, help!
Are you going to sleep all day?

FIRST SOLDIER
(*Wakes and discovers the tomb is empty.*)

Arise, knights and squires!
All of us have slept here too long.

Scandalous things have happened to us;
Jesus has arisen!
My goods and my honor are lost;
We'll be terribly disgraced.

SECOND SOLDIER
(Waking.)

Alas and alack, I dreamed most unpleasantly.
I know in what way it happened,
But I do not know what I am saying.
Aiah! I told you so beforehand,
But you wouldn't listen to me:
His disciples have come
And have taken the Man away from us!

THIRD SOLDIER

Woe to us, for the sleep we slept!
Oh, that we had not called the watchman!
We just felt too sure of him!
Of course, I once read in a book
That a man should never be too sure of anything!
That certainly has been proved now.
Someone tell me, how can we save our honor
When we must appear before Pilate
Now that we have lost Jesus?

FOURTH SOLDIER

Well, lost is lost! Why shout?
Even though things went wrong
We shall insist on our innocence.
Why should we be exiled from this land?
We shall anticipate the situation in a clever way.

We shall appear before Caiaphas
And let the priests know what we think.
   (*They go to the synagogue in the transept left.*)

FIRST SOLDIER

Grace, Lord Bishop!

CAIAPHAS

My heroes, speak up;
How did things go with you?
Have you guarded the tomb well?

SECOND SOLDIER

Lord Bishop, may we speak with impunity?

CAIAPHAS

Tell whatever you know.

FIRST SOLDIER

Lord, believe me this:
In this very night
We were brought to a fearful pass.
Before dawn came
We were struck to the ground
By a mighty earthquake
That brought us to the brink of death.

CAIAPHAS

Come now, up and away with you!
Imagine you great heroes!
Couldn't you at least have run away
And told us about it?

Then we would have placed more men by the tomb.
Couldn't one of you have bucked up the other?

SECOND SOLDIER

Caiaphas, now listen to me!
If this same thing had happened to you,
You would certainly leave off your scolding.
Caiaphas, you ought to be told;
Jesus is not in the grave,
He is risen
And has gone to Galilee.

ANNAS

Just listen to this monkey!
How could a man arise from the dead
Or walk out of his grave?

FOURTH SOLDIER

Annas, you stupid man,
Drop this kind of talk.
I tell the truth.
An angel from the bright heavens
Came with a great light
To the grave and spoke thus:
"Jesus of Nazareth,
He is risen
And has gone to Galilee!"
We don't give a fig for your mockery.
If you want to investigate,
You will find the grave undisturbed.
The angel has lifted off the stone.
It cannot be otherwise but that
God has conquered death's sting.

CAIAPHAS

(CAIAPHAS, ANNAS *and the others hold a brief council.*
ANNAS *begins to write.*)

You knights and trusty heroes!
Look here, take this money
And keep silence regarding all matter
That you heard by the grave.
Should someone ask you where the corpse is,
Then say (you should believe me, in this):
"His disciples have stolen Him out of the grave."
Then these things will remain hidden.

FIRST SOLDIER

We shall keep absolutely still.
Only if Pilate wishes to know this,
Then we must tell him about it
From the very beginning to the end.

ANNAS

Good knights, if you cherish Pilate's favor
Then take with you this letter
And let him have it read;
Then all will end well for you.
　(*He hands the letter to the* FIRST SOLDIER.)

(*The* SOLDIERS *leave for their station at the tomb.
Meanwhile* PILATE *speaks:*)

PILATE

Page, page!

SERVANT

What do you want, my dear lord?

PILATE

Page, go to the grave,
And bring me the latest news.
And tell the knights,
They are to come to their lord.

SERVANT

Lord, that shall be.
                    (*He runs to the sepulchre.*)
Good knights, God greet all four of you
You are all to come immediately
To Pilate, your lord.

THIRD SOLDIER

Page, what must be, must.
I fear, you heroes, that he will read us a nasty lecture.

FOURTH SOLDIER

Dear companions, let it not disturb you!
What is to happen, has to happen.

FIRST SOLDIER

If we could but read, perhaps this letter
Might reassure us—somewhat.
                    (*They go to* PILATE.)

FOURTH SOLDIER

Grace, Lord King!

PILATE

You knights, how does the matter stand?
What has happened to you?
                    (*The* SOLDIERS *exchange glances.*)
What did you see this night at the grave?

FIRST SOLDIER

Pilate, lord King!
Strange things have happened to us.
Here is news indeed,
Great and most important:
Jesus, Whom your soldiers
Were to guard, He is risen.

PILATE

Yes, I should have known that beforehand.
Surely, you have cravenly lost that Man.

SECOND SOLDIER
(*Humbly*.)

Yes, Lord Pilate, that is so.

PILATE

Knights, just how this came about,
You must now report to me.

SECOND SOLDIER

Pilate, from the highest throne
There came beautiful angels;
They took the Man away from us.
Lord, believe me, if you will;
It was not altogether our fault.
As we were lying close to the grave
(Where we could see everything quite plainly),
The angels came in great force.
They robbed us of our wit and senses
And caused us to fall into a sleep.
And they took Jesus out.

With great joy, it seemed to me,
They led Him to a bright spot,
All of which I noticed in my sleep.

PILATE

If you were asleep, how could you see it?
That cannot possibly make sense.
When I see something, then I'm not asleep.
You have, yourselves, between you, invented that story.
And have you slept enough now?
The thumb screws ought to be applied to you.
        (*The* SOLDIERS *wince.*)
You are a fine set of knights!
Utterly lacking in manhood!
You don't any of you deserve a penny's worth of bread.
You are heroes only in running away!
Sit down and let the thumb screws be applied.

THIRD SOLDIER
(*As the* SOLDIERS *look at one another in fear.*)

See, that's what we get for it,
For having gone to sleep by the grave,
Where we were supposed to be on guard!

FIRST SOLDIER
(*To the* FOURTH.)

Be still! All is not yet lost.
        (*To* PILATE.)
My lord, will you be so kind
As to have this letter read?
It bears upon the doings of this night.

PILATE

Here, page, read me this letter.

SERVANT

Lord, I am ever at your service.
                    (*Taking the letter.*)
"Lord Pilate, greetings!
Caiaphas, High Priest, and Annas
Who was formerly High Priest,
And all your people in this land,
They vow to you, Lord King,
Their eternal service and wish you lasting peace.
Therefore, that there may *be* such lasting peace,
They ask of you this petition:
That these four knights
You may receive again straightway
Back into your good graces.
For that they'll ever be in your debt."

PILATE

I see.
Knights, in conformity with this petition
I shall take you back into my service.
I understand. The priests have done a foolish thing.
In bringing about Jesus' death.
They have gained for themselves eternal suffering.
Jesus, who had come from God,
He has risen from the dead.
Now they would like to have it hushed up.
                    (*Loudly.*)
I myself would gladly have saved His life.
Come, let us ponder this most wondrous happening.

(The SOLDIERS *and* SERVANT *follow* PILATE *out the transept doors. Meanwhile* JESUS *and the* ANGELS *reappear in the transept. A portion of the* CHOIR, *which is in the stalls, begins to hum a triumphant Resurrection hymn.)*

FIRST ANGEL

Now comes our praised Lord.
He shall break the gates of brass.
He shall break down those doors
And entirely destroy them.
Son of God, now do this,
Redeem your own people,
Since they are in pain.

SECOND ANGEL

Come and lead the captives from prison,
Sitting in darkness and the shadow of death.

*(*JESUS *follows the two* ANGELS *down the nave, all three joyous. After a distance*:)*

FIRST ANGEL
(Loudly.)

He is going to redeem you in this hour
Out of the pit of that bitter hell.
Therefore, sing aloud!
To welcome the Eternal King.

(From the vestry a portion of the CHOIR, *representing the souls in Hell*:)*

CHOIR
(Chanting.)

Thou hast come, O Desired One, Whom we were waiting
in darkness,

That Thou might this night lead from prison those en-
chained.

(*Reaching the doors, the two* ANGELS *stand aside.*
JESUS *stands before it.*)

JESUS

O prince of darkness, open up this gate!
The King of Glory stands before it!

A DEEP VOICE

(*Representing* LUCIFER, *from beyond the doors.*)

Who is this King of Glory?

JESUS

The Lord, strong and mighty,
The Lord, mighty in battle!

(*In a loud voice.*)

My people shall be free!

(*He throws open the doors. The* CHOIR *beyond breaks
into a triumphant hymn. They are joined by the*
CHOIR *in the stalls, then by the congregation. The
doors close.*)

PLAYS FOR
Other Occasions

The Raising of Lazarus

By Hilarius

CHARACTERS:

Mary
Martha
Two Friends
Jesus

Thomas
First Disciple
Mourners
Lazarus

The Choir

THE SCENE:

Three places are represented. In the transept left is a
platform, the house of LAZARUS in Judea. He is lying
on a cot. By the cot are MARY and MARTHA and TWO
FRIENDS. Transept right represents a place in Galilee;
there, JESUS is seated with two DISCIPLES standing by
Him. The tomb of LAZARUS occupies the chancel. The
CHOIR is in its place.

[*Playing time: 12 minutes.*]

MARY

O, Lazarus, brother, you're so ill!
O fate is hard, indeed.
I, too, am ill for your sweet sake,
Your health my greatest need!

MARTHA

O, bitter fate, so harsh and cruel,
Revoke your grim decree!
But mercy comes from You alone,
O God, we turn to Thee!

FIRST FRIEND

Mary, Martha, cease your weeping,
And kneel to God to pray.

SECOND FRIEND

Perhaps there is some help in Heaven
For the sorrow of this day.

MARY

Go, friends, go to our loving Master,
Go swiftly to the King of Men,
So He may know our brother's state
And come and make him well again.
    (*Music. The* FRIENDS *go to* JESUS *who is seated with
    the* DISCIPLES.)

SECOND FRIEND

Because one dear to You
Is sick and sorely so,
We have been asked to hurry here
As fast as we could go.

FIRST FRIEND

He is upon the point of death,
So come with us, we pray,
That he may live to serve You well
In his old, faithful way.

JESUS

It is not true that he must die,
Although he does seem deathly ill.
Return again and you shall see
How God makes manifest His will.

(*There is mournful music during the following pan-*
tomime:
As the two FRIENDS *leave* JESUS, *the* MOURNERS *come*
in from the left transept door and surround the bed of
LAZARUS. *They pick up the body of* LAZARUS *who*
now is dead, and carry it in solemn procession to the
tomb, in the chancel. The two FRIENDS *meet the pro-*
cession at the crossing and join it, supporting MARY
and MARTHA, *who are walking at the head of it. Dur-*
ing the following four speeches the body is taken to
the tomb, laid within and prepared as in burial.)

MARY

Man is but a mortal now
And feels the sin upon his brow
Of Adam's ancient, broken vow.
Alas, I mourn!
My brother is dead,
I weep forlorn!

FIRST FRIEND

O, put aside these piteous groans,
Let sorrow end, and moans,
Let all this sighing cease.
Let mournful cries,
Sad tears and sighs,
Give way to inward peace.

MARTHA

O, hateful Death,
Detestable Death!
O Death! I grieve!
My brother is dead;
How can I live?

SECOND FRIEND

A soul cannot return and live,
Because his sisters mourn and grieve.
These lamentations that you make
Small help will be.
So cease your tears, for he
Is dead and will not wake.
    (*Musical interlude.*
    The scene shifts to JESUS. *The* MOURNERS *meanwhile*
    take their places with the CHOIR, *but* MARY, MARTHA
    and the two FRIENDS *remain to watch by the grave.*)

JESUS
(*To the* DISCIPLES, *one of whom is* THOMAS.)

We now must go to Judea again
Where I must perform a wonder for men.

FIRST DISCIPLE

But the men of Judea just sought to slay you,
Do not return to their land, I pray you.

JESUS

Lazarus is dead indeed.
There in Judea his sisters grieve,

But this is part of God's great plan,
That men may see and so believe.

THOMAS
(Shrugs.)

Let us go to Judea then,
And risk the anger of those men.
> (*Musical interlude during which* JESUS *and the two*
> DISCIPLES *go to the tomb.* MARTHA *and* MARY *meet*
> JESUS *near the tomb on the chancel steps.*)

MARTHA

Had we, my Lord, had you at call,
    Ah, hence my sorrow!
My brother had not died at all.
    Sweet brother, I have lost you!

Whatever for the living you'd have done
    Ah, hence my sorrow!
Do now for this one dead and gone.
    Sweet brother, I have lost you!

But this I know, that even now,
    Ah, hence my sorrow,
What pure hearts ask, God will allow.
    Sweet brother, I have lost you!

JESUS

Yes, good sister, don't despair:
I am the true life, I am He.
Even your brother lying there
Can live if you believe in me.

And who alive believes in me,
Death will not harm his dying eyes.
Martha, will you believe and see
That in this world new worlds arise?

MARTHA

You, O Christ, of God the Son,
To this our exile You have come
To help us all; Your will be done:
So I believe.

MARY

No one can with consolation
Take from me my desolation,
My sorrow never.
Yet the Son of God, I know,
Can console us here below.
He rules forever.

Therefore You who mighty art,
Gentle, merciful of heart,
Come to the tomb today;
Make my brother live again
Whom the Slayer of the slain
Has taken away.

JESUS

Sister, bring me to the place
Where he is held in Death's embrace.

MARY

(*Leads* JESUS *to the tomb.*)

Behold, Lord, the place
Where Lazarus lies.

In the Father's name,
Let our brother rise.

JESUS
(*Raising his eyes, prays:*)

Father, Your Word and Will display;
Oh, Lord, make Lazarus live, I pray.
So, Father, make known to the world today
    Your Son on earth.

I have not said this to try Your might
But to bring this people into light
That they, made certain by this sight,
    Shall now believe.
        (*Addressing the tomb.*)
Arise, O Lazarus, from the tomb,
And now the gift of life assume.
By virtue of our Father's might,
Come forth again to life and light.
    (LAZARUS *rises and leaves the tomb.*)
Behold, he lives, who once was dead!
Loosen his cerements. Death has fled!

LAZARUS

Behold the works of God, His mighty Will!
Death trembles at His word, and all grows still.
    (*Turns to* JESUS.)
You, Master, You are the King, the Lord of all,
You shall wipe the people's sins away
Obedience to Your behest we pay;
Your kingdom shall not fall.
  (*The* CHOIR *forms a living curtain in front of them,
singing a hymn of praise, while the actors leave by the
chancel door.*)

The Sacrifice of Isaac

CHARACTERS:

Abraham	*An Angel*
Isaac	*Epilogue*
God	*The Choir*

THE SCENE:

The scene in the chancel represents a hilltop in the Promised Land. There is a sacrificial altar center.* ABRAHAM and ISAAC enter from the door at the transept right. They advance to the crossing where ABRAHAM raises his arms and speaks.

[*Playing time*: *25 minutes*.]

ABRAHAM

Omnipotent Father of Heaven!
With all my heart to You I call.
You've given me both land and wealth,
And sent me, too, my livelihood.
Humbly, I thank You for it all.

You fashioned Adam first from clay,
And Eve as well, to be his wife;
All other creatures sprang from them.

* See Production Notes, p. 258.

And You've allowed Your Abraham
Here in this land to lead his life.

And granted me in my old age
This sweet, young child with me to dwell;
Isaac here, my own fair son,
Means more to me than anyone,
Save for Yourself, Whom I love so well!

True, I have other children, too,
But them I hold not half so dear;
He cheers me so, this fair, sweet child!
No matter where I chance to go,
Grief is a stranger to me here.

And therefore, Father, now I pray
For Isaac's health and for his grace;
Oh, Lord, protect him night and day,
That neither sorrow, harm nor fear
Shall touch my child in any place.

Now, Isaac, come, my own sweet child,
We shall go home and take our rest.

ISAAC

Father, you are so gentle with me;
I'm always ready to do
Whatever you think best.

ABRAHAM

(*Putting his arm around* ISAAC'S *shoulders.*)

Of all the children in my house,
I know you are the worthiest.
    (*They cross to the transept left.*)

GOD

(*In the chancel. Speaks to his* ANGEL.)

My angel, hurry on your way.
Go down at once to middle-earth.
I mean to test my Abram's heart,
And see how much his vows are worth.

Say I commanded him to take
Isaac, the son he loves so well,
And sacrifice his blood to me,
If he would keep my friendship still.

Show him the way up to the hill
Where Isaac's sacrifice shall be.
The time has come to try his heart,
Whom he loves better—his child or me.

All men shall learn this rule from him:
Accept your Maker's sovereignty!

> (GOD *leaves through the chancel door.* ABRAHAM *returns to the crossing alone, leaving* ISAAC *kneeling in the left transept.* ABRAHAM *kneels in prayer. The* ANGEL *comes to stand above him on the chancel steps.*)

ABRAHAM

I make my prayers to you again,
Father in Heaven, Maker of everything.
For on this day I offer up
The sacrifice prescribed by law,
Almighty God, my Lord and King.

What creature must I kill?
If I could know,

It should be done with all my strength,
And quickly, too.
To do your pleasure on a hill,
Dear Father, God in Trinity,
Verily it is my will!

ANGEL

(From the chancel steps.)

Abraham! Abraham!
Would you know peace?
Our Lord commands you now, obey!
Take Isaac, your beloved son,
And offer up his blood today.

Go now into the Land of Vision
Where God prescribes that you must yield.
I'll lead you there and show the place.
Submit yourself to God's decree.
Follow me now across this field.

ABRAHAM

I welcome you, God's messenger,
And I will do as you decree.
Yet Isaac, my young son, has been
A dear, obedient child to me.

And so I'd rather, had God been pleased,
Have given up *my* worldly station,
Than that my Isaac should be dead,
If it could win my soul's salvation.

There's none on earth I love so much,
Yet I must carry out the task.

Lord God, my heart is deeply stirred,
And yet, dear Lord, I am afraid
To grudge You anything You ask.

I love my child as I do life,
But yet I love my God much more.
For though my heart would fight for them,
I would not spare my child or wife,
No matter how they might implore.

I love my son so well—so well—
Yet soon the boy shall feel my sword.
Ah, Father in Heaven, behold, I kneel!
My son shall meet a bitter death
To honor You, O Lord!

ANGEL

Abraham, Abraham, this is well said!
And keep His commandments day and night;
But in your heart be not dismayed.

ABRAHAM

No, no, in truth I am well paid
By pleasing God with all my might.

For though my heart will suffer much
To carry out this dreadful deed,
For all of that I'll not hold back,
But I will go and fetch him now,
And we'll return with all our speed.

(The ANGEL *leaves by the chancel door.* ABRAHAM
crosses to the transept left where ISAAC *is kneeling in
prayer.*)

The Sacrifice of Isaac

Isaac, my son, where are you, child?
Your father's calling; speak to me.

ISAAC

Father, sweet father, here I am,
Making my prayers to the Trinity.

ABRAHAM

Get up, my son, and come with me;
My gentle lad, who is so wise.
We two must go together, child,
And make our holy sacrifice.

ISAAC

I'm ready, father, by your side.
No matter what you ask of me,
I'll do the very best I can
At once and cheerfully.

ABRAHAM

Ah, Isaac, son—my dear, sweet child,
God's blessings on you, and mine as well.
            (*He picks up a bundle of faggots.*)
These faggots—put them on your back,
And I, myself, shall bring the fire.

ISAAC

Yes, father, I'll carry them to the hill;
I'm eager to do
Whatever you will.

ABRAHAM
(Aside.)

Lord, never has man been tempted so
To disobey—not since the Fall.
                    (To ISAAC.*)*
Now Isaac, son, let's go our way
Onto that hill. Let's hurry. Come.
    (They go toward ABRAHAM'S *sacrificial altar which is
    placed in the center of the chancel.)*

ISAAC

I'm coming, father, but you are so tall.
Though I'm eager to follow,
It's hard, I'm so small.

ABRAHAM
(Aside.)

Ah, Lord, my heart! What pain for me!
This infant speaks so lovingly.
            (They arrive at the sacrificial altar.)

No need to hold those any longer,
So lay the faggots on the ground.
For I must make all ready now
To honor God, as I am bound.

ISAAC

Yes, father. There—I've put them down.
            (He lays down the faggots.)
I'll stay by you to give you cheer.
But, father, it seems very strange
For you to be as sad as you appear.

And, father, I am growing frightened;
Where's the live beast that you should kill?
We have the fire here, and wood,
But there's no offering on this hill.

I know a creature must be killed
To make a proper sacrifice.

ABRAHAM

Don't be afraid, I tell you, child.
Our Lord will send, by His sweet angel,
Some living thing that will suffice.

ISAAC

Yes, father, but my heart is trembling
To see that sharp sword in your hand.
Why do you hold your sword like that,
And look so stern? I cannot understand.

ABRAHAM
(Aside.)

Oh, Lord above, what shall I do?
This infant breaks my heart in two!

ISAAC

Do you intend your sword for me?
Father, please tell me, if you will.

ABRAHAM

I swear you break my heart to bits!
My Isaac, son, be still, be still!

ISAAC

Father, truly it seems to me
That you are mourning more and more.

ABRAHAM
(*Aside.*)

Oh, God, have mercy! Send me Your grace!
My heart was never half so sore!

ISAAC

Do you mean me any harm?
I beg you, father, make it plain!

ABRAHAM

Sweet son, I cannot tell you yet,
My heart is now so full of pain.

ISAAC

Dear father, do not hide it from me.
Do you mean evil to your son?

ABRAHAM

Ah, Isaac, Isaac—I must kill you!

ISAAC

Kill me? Why? What have I done?

If I have disobeyed your will,
A rod would quickly make me mild;
But don't destroy me with your sword,
For am I not your well-loved child?

The Sacrifice of Isaac

ABRAHAM

It grieves me, son, to shed your blood.
But there's Another I must please.

ISAAC

Would God my mother were here now
To plead for me upon her knees.

And save my life.
But since my mother is not here,
I beg you, father, change your mind
And do not kill me with your knife.

ABRAHAM

I have not any choice in this,
And all your prayers I cannot heed.
It's God's commandment, and His will,
That I should carry out this deed.

He has commanded me Himself
To see this sacrifice is done.

ISAAC

Is it God's will I should be slain?

ABRAHAM

Yes, truly, Isaac, my good son,
And so my heart is full of pain.

ISAAC

Dear father, I will never go
Against God's will in any measure.

He might have sent a better fate
If it had only been His pleasure.

ABRAHAM

I know, but if I failed in this,
He would regard me angrily.

ISAAC

No, no, my father, God forbid
That you should grieve Him so for me.

You've other children—one or two—
Whom you by nature ought to love.
I beg you, father, don't be sad,
For when I once am dead to you,
You'll soon forget the son you had.

So therefore carry out His will,
And when I'm dead, then pray for me.
But, father, tell my mother nothing;
Just say that I have gone away.

ABRAHAM

O Isaac, blessed may you be!

My heart begins to tremble now
That I must see my Isaac die.

ISAAC

Oh, father, since it must be done,
Let's do it calmly, you and I.

But bless me in a gentle breath,
Before I go to meet my death.

              (ISAAC *kneels.*)

ABRAHAM

With all my strength then, son, receive
My blessings on you in this place,
And God will bless you, too, I know.
Oh, Isaac, Isaac, son! Stand up!
So I may kiss your fair, sweet face!

ISAAC

Farewell, my gentle, loving father,
And say farewell to mother, too.
And, father, hide my eyes.
So I don't see your sword come down
And cut my flesh, I beg of you.

ABRAHAM

Oh, son, I weep at every word;
Now, speak no more, my dear.

ISAAC

But why, my own dear father, why?
We won't be long together here.

And since I must be killed today,
I beg you: strike but one quick blow
To make a speedy end of it;
It will be better so.

ABRAHAM

Your gentle words all but destroy
My strength to do this dreadful thing,

And yet I must obey God's will.
Ah, Isaac, child, my own sweet boy,
Come kiss your father once again.
Most faithful child, you are my joy!

ISAAC

Oh, father, please don't wait so long!
But listen to your Isaac's plea!
I beg you, father, make an end!

ABRAHAM

Come close, my son, come close to me.

(ABRAHAM *starts to bind* ISAAC'*s hands.*)
I have to tie your hands together,
Although your temper is so mild.

ISAAC

Ah, mercy, father! Why do that?

ABRAHAM

So you won't try to stop me, child.

ISAAC

No, no! I swear I won't do that!
Go on and carry out your will,
And, for the blessed love of God,
The purpose that you have, fulfill.

I do not wish to die today,
But still my God I would not grieve.
So sternly carry out your will,
My father dear, I give you leave.

But let me beg you now to tell
My mother nothing, once again.
If she should hear it, she would weep.
I think she loves me very well.
May God protect her from all pain!

So now, farewell, my dear, sweet mother.
We'll never meet again, I know.

ABRAHAM

Ah, Isaac, son, you make me weep,
And fill my aching heart with woe!

ISAAC

I'm sorry, father, if I grieve you.
Forgive me, please, for what I've done.
And for all my trespasses allow
Forgiveness, too, when I am gone!
God in Heaven, be with me now!

ABRAHAM

Ah, child! Leave off repenting, do!
In all your life you've never grieved me.
No—blessings on you, through and through,
For being bred to me and born.
You've been the best of all my children.
But, child, no matter how I mourn,

No matter how I grieve, I still
Must shed your blood upon this hill.

And so, my son, here you must lie.
                (*He places* ISAAC *on the altar.*)
And now I must begin my work.

I wish I were the one to die.
If it would please the Deity,
I'd offer up myself instead.

ISAAC

Oh, father, please don't mourn for me.

Your weeping makes my heart as sore
As my own death, and even more.

Your kerchief, father—oh, please bind
My eyes!

ABRAHAM

I will, my sweetest child.

ISAAC

And, once again, keep this in mind:
Don't strike me often with your sword,
But do it quickly, so it's done.

ABRAHAM
(*Laying a cloth over* ISAAC'*s face.*)

Farewell, child, Chosen of the Lord!

ISAAC

Dear father, let me lie face down,
For I am frightened of your sword.

ABRAHAM
(*Aside.*)

It wrings my heart to do this deed,
But, Lord, Your will I'll not withstand.

ISAAC

My Father in Heaven, to you I cry!
Receive my soul into Your hand!

ABRAHAM
(Aside.)

The time has come for certain now,
My sword must fall upon his neck.
My heart rebels against my vow.
My weakness holds the blow in check.
It goes against my very grain,
And yet I want to do Your will.
But this young innocent lies so still
I may not *ever* have the strength.
Oh, Father, help me in my pain!

ISAAC

Mercy, father, why do you wait?
All this while you let me lie!
I wish you would not hesitate.
I beg you, father, end my anguish;
Don't let me wait like this to die!

ABRAHAM

My heart, my heart, why don't you break?
And still I will not be beguiled!
I'll wait no more for your sweet sake,
Because my God would be aggrieved.
Now—take the blow, my own dear child!
(ABRAHAM *draws back to strike, but the* ANGEL, *who has come from the chancel door, suddenly takes the sword in his hand.*)

ANGEL

I am an Angel, as you see,
Sent down to stay your hand.
Our Lord thanks you a hundred times
For obeying His command.

He knows your will. He knows your heart
Fears Him as few men do.
And to relieve your heavy thoughts,
I've brought a ram for you.

(*Points behind the choir stalls.*)

Look there, he's tied among the briars.
Now, Abraham, good cheer,
For you shall not be forced to shed
The blood of one so dear.

Go, make the ram your offering.
Farewell, O man of loyalty.
For I go home to Heaven's King,
To bask in His Divinity.
Lift Isaac up. Your son is free.

(*The* ANGEL *leaves as he came.*)

ABRAHAM

Now I am eased in many ways!
Oh, Lord, I thank You for Your grace!
Rise up, my Isaac, my dear son!
Rise up, sweet child, and lift your face!

ISAAC

Ah, mercy! Please! Why don't you strike?
Ah, father! Strike me with your knife!

The Sacrifice of Isaac

ABRAHAM

Peace, my sweet son, forget your fears.
Through His good angel messenger
Our Lord has spared your life.
And you'll not die today, my son.

ISAAC

Ah, father, I'd be happy, too,—
I would—father—I say—I would—
If this were true.

ABRAHAM

I'll kiss you now an hundred times
For joy! My fair young son, so good!

ISAAC

Won't this draw down God's anger
On us, dear father Abraham?

ABRAHAM

No, no, I hardly think so, son,
For He has sent that ram.

(He points behind the choir stalls.)
The beast shall die instead of you,
In honor of our Lord today.
Go, bring him over here, my child.

ISAAC

I'll go and take him by the horns,
And bring him to you right away.

(ISAAC *gets the ram.*)
Ah, sheep, my sheep! His blessings on you
For setting me at liberty!
Yes, you shall die for me today
In worship of the Trinity.
Now, come along. We'll go together
To my Father in Heaven, we two.
Although it means you lose your head,
I still would rather it were you
Than I whose blood was shed.

(*He brings the ram to his father.*)
Look here, how quickly I have brought
This gentle sheep. He is for you.
I thank You, Lord, for what You've wrought,
And I am glad that I shall live,
And once again shall kiss my mother.

ABRAHAM

Come now, be merry, Isaac, do;
For this obedient beast you give
Shall be the sacrifice, no other.

ISAAC

And I will blow the fire up
So it will burn and burn and burn!
(*He hesitates.*)
But, father, now I dare not stoop.
You will not kill me if I turn?

ABRAHAM

No, hardly, son. All that is past;
You need not be dismayed.

The Sacrifice of Isaac

ISAAC

(Kneeling and appearing to blow on the fire while ABRAHAM *prepares to sacrifice the ram.)*

I wish that sword were in the fire,
For I am still afraid.

*(*ABRAHAM *appears to slay the ram and make his offering. He kneels beside* ISAAC.)*

ABRAHAM

Almighty God, Omnipotent!
Lord God of Heaven in Trinity!
I make the offering which you sent.
Accept my meaning in this place,
As I present this living beast,
And You are God—Giver of grace!

(He and ISAAC *bow their heads in silent prayer.)*
*(*GOD *enters the chancel behind the two, and stands farther away back of them where they do not see him.)*

GOD

Abraham! Abraham!
You shall know bliss!
And Isaac, the son at your side!
Abraham, know that for this
You shall multiply, Isaac and you,
As thick as the stars that abide;
And as thick as the sands of the sea
You shall multiply, Isaac and you!
I grant you this gift, because you are true!

Numberless sons shall spring forth from you,
And eternal bliss they shall know.

For you fear only me as your God,
And keep my every commandment.
I give you my blessing wherever you go!
   (GOD *lifts his arms in the air for an instant and leaves
   through the chancel door.*)

ABRAHAM
(*Rises.*)

Now Isaac, son, what do you think
Of what we've done here, you and I?
We can be happy now that we
On this fair hill did not the will
Of God deny.

ISAAC
(*Rises.*)

I thank our Lord in every way
That I was wise enough to fear
The wrath of God much more than death.

ABRAHAM

Why, my good son, were you afraid?
Speak up and let me hear.

ISAAC

Yes, father, I can tell you now,
I was never so afraid as then,
Right here upon this hill;
And, by my faith, I make a vow:
I never will come here again,
Except against my will.

The Sacrifice of Isaac

ABRAHAM

That's right, my son, we're going home,
And quickly, too, so come with me.

ISAAC

I'm ready, by my faith, dear father.
I never was so glad to go and see
And speak with my dear mother.

ABRAHAM

O Lord of Heaven, thanks to You,
That now I may take home with me
My son, my Isaac, free and fair,
The gentlest child You'll ever see,
As I can truly swear!

Now let's go home, my blessed son.

ISAAC

All right, dear father, let us go,
For, as I live, now this is done
Never again will I come here.
I pray God's grace on us forever,
And on all those whom we hold dear.

(ABRAHAM *and* ISAAC *leave by the transept left. The*
EPILOGUE *enters through the chancel door and advances
to the chancel steps.*)

EPILOGUE
(*Addressing the congregation.*)

And so, sweet gentlefolk, we've shown
This solemn story to great and small.

It holds a lesson for the fool
And for the wisest of us all—
Yes, all of us—bar none.
For this brief story shows us here
How we should keep, yes every one,
The Lord's commandments without fear.

Imagine God had sent an angel
Commanding you your child to kill.
Do you believe there's one of you
Who'd not begrudge His holy will?
Think now, would you be faithful still?

I doubt there would be many.
And of those women who weep and groan,
When God has taken a child of their own,
There hardly would be any.
I tell you it is only mad
To grudge your God or moan your fate;
For He's your Lord, remember that
Before it is too late!

And don't complain against our Lord,
In wealth or woe, whichever He send;
No matter what your state afford;
For when He wishes, He can mend,
If you have truly done His will,
As you have seen in our short play.
And if you're safe—why, serve Him still,
That you may please Him night and day.

Now, Christ, betrayed by traitor's kiss,
Bring us all to Heaven's bliss!

   (*The* EPILOGUE *leaves as he came. The* CHOIR *and congregation join in singing an appropriate hymn of praise.*)

The Tragedy of Job

CHARACTERS:

Narrator	*Zophar the Naamathite*
Job	*Elihu the Buzite,*
Eliphaz the Temanite	*a young man*
Bildad the Shuhite	*The Chorus*
	The Voice

THE SCENE:

Outside the ruins of Job's house. These may be indicated by a single, scorched column, still standing after the house was razed by fire, at the extreme right side of the chancel, or it may not be indicated at all. Slightly to the left of the center of the chancel is a sacrificial altar.

At the beginning of the play the NARRATOR enters from the chancel door. He ascends to the pulpit where he remains throughout the play. He is soon followed by JOB, who comes in from the chancel door. He is clothed in rags and wasted by disease. Leaning heavily on a stick, he goes to the top step leading to the chancel. Here he sits down, hiding his head in his arms.

[*Playing time: 45 minutes.*]

NARRATOR

(*Reading from a big book.*)

There was a man in the land of Uz, whose name was Job; and that man was perfect and upright, and one that feared

God, and turned away from evil. And there were born unto
him seven sons and three daughters. His substance was also
seven thousand sheep, and three thousand camels, and five
hundred yoke of oxen, and five hundred she-asses, and a
very great household; so that this man was the greatest of
all the children of the east.

Now it came to pass on the day when the sons of God came
to present themselves before Jehovah, that Satan also came
among them. And Jehovah said unto Satan, "Hast thou considered my servant Job? for there is none like him in the
earth, a perfect and upright man, one that feareth God, and
turneth away from evil." Then Satan answered Jehovah,
and said, "Does Job fear God for nought? Hast not Thou
made a hedge about him, and about his house, and about all
that he hath, on every side? Thou hast blessed the work of
his hands, and his substance is increased in the land. But put
forth Thy hand now, and touch all that he hath and he will
renounce Thee to Thy face!" And Jehovah said unto Satan,
"Behold, all that he hath is in thy power; only upon himself put not forth thy hand." So Satan went forth from the
presence of Jehovah.

And it fell on a day when his sons and his daughters were
eating and drinking wine in their eldest brother's house, that
there came a messenger unto Job, and said, "The oxen were
plowing, and the asses feeding beside them; and the Sabæans
fell upon them, and took them away: yea; they have slain
the servants with the edge of the sword; and I only am
escaped alone to tell thee." While he was yet speaking, there
came also another, and said: "The fire of God is fallen from
heaven; and hath burned up the sheep and the servants, and

consumed them; and I only am escaped to tell thee." While
he was yet speaking there came also another, and said: "The
Chaldeans made three bands, and fell upon the camels, and
have taken them away, yea, and slain the servants with the
edge of the sword; and I only am escaped to tell thee." While
he was yet speaking there came also another, and said: "Thy
sons and thy daughters were eating and drinking wine in
their eldest brother's house; and, behold, there came a great
wind from the wilderness, and smote the four corners of the
house, and it fell upon the young men and they are dead;
and I only am escaped alone to tell thee."

Then Job arose, and rent his robe, and shaved his head, and
fell down upon the ground, and worshipped; and he said,
"Naked came I out of my mother's womb, and naked shall I
return thither; Jehovah gave and Jehovah hath taken away;
blessed be the name of Jehovah!" In all this Job sinned not,
nor charged God foolishly.

Again it came to pass on the day when the sons of God came
to present themselves before Jehovah, that Satan came also
among them to present himself also before Jehovah. And
Jehovah said unto Satan, "Hast thou considered my servant,
Job? for there is none like him in the earth, a perfect and
an upright man, one that feareth God, and turneth away
from evil: and he still holdeth fast his integrity, although
thou movedest me against him, to destroy him without
cause." And Satan answered Jehovah, and said, "Skin for
skin, yea, all that a man hath will he give for his life. But put
forth Thy hand now, and touch his bone and his flesh, and
he will renounce Thee before Thy face." And Jehovah said
unto Satan, "Behold, he is in thy hands; only spare his life."

So Satan went forth from the presence of Jehovah, and smote Job with sore boils from the sole of his foot unto his crown. And he took him a potsherd to scrape himself therewith; and he sat among the ashes.

Now when Job's three friends heard of all this evil which was come upon him, they came every one from his own place: Eliphaz the Temanite, and Bildad the Shuhite, and Zophar the Naamathite; and they made an appointment together to come to bemoan him and to comfort him. And when they lifted up their eyes afar off, and knew him not, they lifted up their voices, and wept; and they rent everyone his robe, and sprinkled dust upon their heads toward heaven.

(As the NARRATOR *finishes reading the* CHORUS *begins to drift in, two by two and three by three, in little groups, from the transept doors. They converse together in low tones as they pass through the crossing and up the chancel steps. They point* JOB *out to each other as they go by him. They take their places in the choir stalls. They are led by* ELIHU THE BUZITE, *who stands in front of them by the altar. After the* CHORUS *have taken their places* BILDAD *and* ELIPHAZ *enter together from the transept left. They pass to the crossing, below the altar and make their obeisances and then pass to the right of* JOB, *stopping beside him. They are soon followed by* ZOPHAR *who goes through the same ceremonies and then stops to the left of* JOB.)

JOB
(Raising his head.)

Let the day perish wherein I was born;
And the night which said, There is a man child conceived!
Let that day be darkness;

Wherefore is light given to him that is in misery,
And life unto the bitter in soul?
Who long for death, but it cometh not;
And dig for it more than for hidden treasures;
Who rejoice exceedingly
And are glad when they can find the grave.
Why is light given to a man whose way is hid,
And whom God hath hedged in?

For the thing which I fear cometh upon me,
And that which I am afraid of cometh unto me.
I am not at ease, neither am I quiet,
Neither have I rest: but trouble cometh!

CHORUS
(*In unison.*)

The Lord giveth and the Lord taketh away
Blessed be the name of the Lord.

ELIPHAZ

If one assay to commune with thee, wilt thou be grieved? —
But who can withhold himself from speaking?
Behold, thou hast instructed many,
And thou hast strengthened the weak hands.
Thy words have upholden him that was falling,
And thou hast made firm the feeble knees.
But now it is come unto thee, and thou faintest,
It toucheth thee, and thou art troubled.
Is not thy fear of God thy confidence,
And the integrity of thy ways thy hope?

Now a thing was secretly brought to me,
And mine ear receiveth a whisper thereof.

Fear came upon me and trembling,
Which made all my bones to shake.
Then a spirit passed before my face;
The hair of my flesh stood up.
It stood still, but I could not discern the appearance thereof;
A form was before mine eyes:
There was silence, and I heard a voice, saying
"Shall mortal man be more just than God?
Shall a man be more pure than his Maker?"
Behold, he putteth no trust in his servants;
And his angels he chargeth with folly:
How much more them that dwell in houses of clay,
Whose foundation is in the dust,
Who are crushed before the moth!
Betwixt morning and evening they are destroyed;
For affliction cometh not forth from the dust,
Neither doth trouble spring out of the ground;
But a man is born unto trouble,
As sparks fly upward.

But as for me, I would seek God,
And unto God would I commit my cause.
(Very solemnly.)
Happy is the man whom God correcteth:
Therefore despise not thou the chastening of the Almighty.
For He maketh sore, and He bindeth up;
He woundeth, and His hands make whole.
He will deliver thee in six troubles,
Yea, in seven there shall no evil touch thee.
In famine He will redeem thee from death;
And in war from the power of the sword.
Thou shalt be hid from the scourge of the tongue;

Neither shalt thou be afraid of destruction when it cometh.
Lo this, we have searched it, so it is;
Hear it, and know it for thy good.

JOB
(*Rises.*)

Oh that my vexation were but weighed,
And all my calamity laid in the balances!
For now it would be heavier than the sand of the seas!
Therefore have my words been rash.
For the arrows of the Almighty are within me,
The poison whereof my spirit drinketh up:
The terrors of God do set themselves in array against me.
Things that my soul refused to touch,
Lo! they are as my loathsome food.
Oh, that I might have my request,
And that God would grant me the thing that I long for!
Even that it would please God to crush me;
That He would let loose His hand and cut me off!
Then should I yet have comfort;
For what is my strength that I should wait?
And what is mine end, that I should be patient?
Is my strength the strength of stone?
Or is my flesh of brass?
Is it not that I have no hope in me,
And that prosperity is driven quite from me?
(*Placing his hand on* ELIPHAZ's *shoulder.*)
To him that is ready to faint kindness should be showed
     from his friend;
Even to him that forsaketh the fear of the Almighty.
(BILDAD *and* ZOPHAR *turn away.*)
My brethren have dealt deceitfully as a brook.

Ye see a terror, and are afraid.
Did I say, Give unto me?
Or, Offer a present for me of your substance?
Or, Deliver me from the adversary's hand?
Now therefore be pleased to look upon me.
  (*They face him again, reluctantly.* JOB *proceeds with biting incisiveness.*)
My flesh is clothed with worms and clods of dust;
My skin healeth and breaketh out afresh.
My days are swifter than a weaver's shuttle,
And are spent without hope.
Therefore I will not refrain my mouth;
          (*As* ELIPHAZ *offers to silence him.*)
I will speak in the anguish of my spirit;
I will complain in the bitterness of my soul.

          (*Turning toward the altar.*)
I loathe my life;
I would not live alway;
Let me alone,
For my days are vanity.
For what is man, that Thou shouldest magnify him,
And that Thou shouldest visit him every morning,
And try him every moment?
If I have sinned, what do I unto Thee, O thou watcher of
    men?
Why dost Thou not pardon my transgression,
And take away mine iniquity?

BILDAD

How long wilt thou speak these things?
Doth God pervert justice?

If thou wouldest seek diligently unto God
And make thy supplication to the Almighty,
If thou wert pure and upright, surely now He would awake
    for thee,
And make the habitation of thy righteousness prosper.
Apply thyself to that which the fathers have searched out:
Shall not they teach thee and tell thee,
And utter words out of their heart?
Can papyrus grow without mire?
Can the Nile-grass grow without water?
Whilst it is yet in its greenness, and not cut down,
It withereth before any other herb.
So are the paths of all that forget God;
And the hope of the godless man shall perish.
Behold: God will not cast away a perfect man,
Neither will He uphold the evildoers.
He will yet fill thy mouth with laughter.
And thy lips with songs of gladness.
They that hate thee shall be clothed with shame,
And the tent of the wicked shall be no more.

JOB

Of a truth I know that it is so:
But how can man be just with God?
If God be pleased to contend with him,
Man cannot answer Him one in a thousand.
God is wise in heart and mighty in strength:
Who hath hardened himself against Him and prospered?
Him who removeth mountains and they know it not
When He overturneth them in His anger.
Who alone stretcheth out the heavens,
And treadeth upon the waves of the sea.

Who doeth great things past finding out;
Yea, marvellous things without number.

Lo, He goeth by me, and I see Him not:
He glideth on, but I perceive Him not:
Behold, He seizeth the prey, who can hinder Him?
Who will say unto Him, What doest thou?

For Him, though I be righteous, would I have no answer;
Yet Him, my judge, must I supplicate.
For He breaketh me with a tempest,
And multiplieth my wounds without cause.
He will not suffer me to take my breath,
But filleth me with bitterness.

If pestilence slay suddenly,
And the guiltless perish—He laughs.
The earth is given into the hand of the wicked:
He covereth the faces of the judges thereof.
If it be not He,
Who then is it?
           (*The friends hide their faces at the blasphemy.*)

I will give free course to my complaint;
I will speak in the bitterness of my soul.
I will say unto God:
                    (*Toward the altar again.*)
                    Do not condemn me;
Shew me wherefore thou contendest with me.
Is it good unto Thee that Thou shouldest oppress,
That Thou shouldest despise the work of Thine hands.
Thine hands have framed me,

Yet Thou dost destroy me.
Are not my days few?
Cease then, and let me alone,
That I may take comfort a little
Before I go whence I shall not return—
Even to the land of darkness and of the shadow of death.

ZOPHAR
(Indignant, with uplifted hand, to BILDAD *and* ELIPHAZ
who are trying to hold him back.)

Should not the multitude of words be answered?
And should a man full of talk be justified?
(To JOB.)
Should thy boastings make men hold their peace?
And when thou mockest, shall no man make thee ashamed?
For thou sayest, My doctrine is pure,
And I am clean in mine own eyes.
But O that God would speak,
And open his lips against thee;
And that He would show thee the secrets of wisdom;
For He is manifold in understanding!

Know therefore that God exacteth of thee
Less than thine iniquity deserveth.

If He pass through, and imprison,
And bring unto judgment, then who can hinder Him?
For He knoweth false men.

But vain man is void of understanding,
Yea, man is born as a wild ass's colt.
(Pleadingly.)

If thou set thine heart aright,
And stretch out thine hands toward Him;
If iniquity be in thine hand, put it far away,
And let not unrighteousness dwell in thy tents;
Surely then shalt thou lift up thy face without spot;
Yea, thou shalt be stedfast, and shalt not fear;
For thou shalt forget thy misery.

JOB

No doubt but ye are the people,
And wisdom shall die with you.
But I have understanding as well as you;
I am not inferior to you.
(*Ironically.*)
I am as one that is the laughingstock to his neighbor,
I, who called upon God, and He answered,
The just, the perfect man is a laughingstock.

Your memorable sayings are proverbs of ashes,
Your defences are defences of clay.
  (*The* CHORUS *murmurs indignantly;* ELIPHAZ *tries to
  interrupt.*)
Hold your peace, let me alone, that I may speak
And let come on me what will.
Even this shall be my security;
That a hypocrite would not come unto Him.

Hear diligently my speech,
And let my declaration be in your ears.
Behold now, I have set my cause in order:
I know that I am righteous.
(*Challenging all his audience, then God.*)

Who is he that will *refute* me this?
For then would I hold my peace and give up the ghost.
                    (*Advancing toward the altar.*)
Only do not two things unto me,
Then will I not hide myself from Thy face:
Withdraw Thine hand far from me;
And let not Thy terror make me afraid:
Then call Thou, and I will answer;
Or let me speak, and answer Thou me.

How many are mine iniquities and sins?
Make me to know my transgression and my sin.
Wherefore hidest Thou Thy face,
And holdest me for Thine enemy?

My transgression is sealed in a bag,
And Thou fastenest up mine iniquity.

ELIHU
(*At the altar.*)

Where shall wisdom be found?
And where is the place of understanding?

SEMICHORUS I

Surely there is a mine for silver
And a place for gold which they refine.
Iron is taken out of the earth,
And copper is molten out of the stone.
Man setteth an end to darkness
And seeketh out to the farthest bound
The stones from obscurity and thick darkness.

A MEMBER OF THE CHORUS

But where shall wisdom be found?
And where is the place of understanding?

SEMICHORUS II

Man putteth forth his hand upon the flinty rock;
He turneth the mountains by the roots.
He cutteth out channels among the rocks;
He bindeth the streams that they trickle not;
And his eye seeth every precious thing.
And the thing that is hid bringeth he forth to light.

ELIHU

But where shall wisdom be found?
And where is the place of understanding?

SEMICHORUS I

Man knoweth not the price thereof;
Neither is it found in the land of the living.
The deep saith, It is not in me:
And the sea saith, It is not with me.
It cannot be gotten for gold,
Neither shall silver be weighed for the price thereof.

A MEMBER OF THE CHORUS

Whence then cometh wisdom
And where is the place of understanding?
It is hid from the eyes of all living,
And kept close from the fowls of the air!

ELIHU

God understandeth the way thereof,
And He knoweth the place thereof.

For He looketh to the ends of the earth,
Yea, He meteth out the waters by measure.
When He made a decree for rain,
And a way for the lightning of thunder,
Then did He see it and declare it;
He established it, yea, and searched it out.
And unto man said:

FULL CHORUS

Behold, the fear of the Lord, *that* is wisdom,
And to depart from evil is understanding.

ELIPHAZ

Thine own mouth condemneth thee, and not I;
Yea, thine own lips testify against thee.
Art thou the first man that was born?
Or wast thou brought forth before the hills?
Hast thou heard the secret counsel of God?
And dost thou limit wisdom to thyself?
I will show thee, hear thou me;
And that which I have seen I will declare:
The wicked man travaileth with pain all his days,
He knoweth that the day of darkness is ready at his hand:
Distress and anguish make him afraid;
Because he hath stretched out his hand against God,
And behaveth himself proudly against the Almighty;
He shall not be rich, neither shall his substance continue,
Neither shall his possessions be extended on the earth.
By the breath of God's mouth shall he go away.
Let him not trust in vanity, deceiving himself:
For vanity shall be his recompense.

The Tragedy of Job

I have heard many such things:
Miserable comforters are ye all.

(*Toward the altar.*)

Thou hast made desolate all my company.
And Thou hast laid fast hold on me, and the strength of Thy
  grip is taken to be witness against me:
My very leanness riseth up against me, it testifieth to my
  face.

(*To his friends.*)

He hath torn me in His wrath, and persecuted me;
He hath gnashed upon me with His teeth:
Mine adversary sharpeneth his eyes upon me.
They have gaped upon me with their mouth;
They have smitten me upon the cheek reproachfully:
They gather themselves together against me.
God delivereth me to the ungodly,
And casteth me into the hands of the wicked.
My face is foul with weeping,
And on my eyelids is the shadow of death;
—Although there is no violence in mine hands,
And my prayer is pure.

(*He pauses a minute—the* FRIENDS *smile mockingly. He
  continues, enraged.*)

O earth, cover not thou my blood,
And let my cry have no resting place!
My friends scoff at me
But even now, behold, my witness is in heaven,

(*The* FRIENDS *laugh quietly.*)

And He that voucheth for me is on high.

(*The* FRIENDS *laugh aloud.* JOB *turns toward the altar.*)

Give now a pledge, be surety for me Thyself;

Who else is there that will strike hands with me?
            (*Sweeping the scene in appeal.*)
For Thou hast hid their heart from understanding:
Therefore shalt Thou not exalt them.
                    (*To the* FRIENDS.)
He that denounceth his friends for a prey,
Even the eyes of his children shall fail.
      (ZOPHAR *spits at him, while others grunt* "Sinner! Liar!
      Enemy of God!")
He hath made me also a byword of the people;
And they spit in my face.

BILDAD
            (*Interrupting angrily.*)
Wherefore are we counted as beasts,
And are become unclean in thy sight?
Thou that tearest thyself in thine anger,
Shall the earth be forsaken for thee?
Or shall the rock be removed out of its place?
      (*The* CHORUS *makes a menacing movement toward*
      JOB.)

JOB
I find not a wise man among you:
Upright men shall be astonished at this
And the pure shall bestir themselves against the hypocrites.
Yes, the righteous man *shall* yet hold on his way:
And he that is clean of hands shall wax stronger and
      stronger!

BILDAD
      (*Talking him down, taking the words out of his
      mouth.*)
Yea, the light of the wicked *shall* be put out,
And the spark of his fire shall *not* shine.

For he is cast into a net by his own feet,
And he walketh upon the toils.
A gin shall take him by the heel,
And a snare shall lay hold on him.
He shall have neither son nor son's son among his people,
Nor any remaining where he sojourned.
Surely such are the dwellings of the unrighteous,
And this is the place of him that knoweth not God.

JOB

These ten times have ye reproached me:
And be it indeed that I have erred,
Mine error remaineth with myself.
If indeed ye *will* magnify yourselves against me,
And plead against me my reproach,
Know then that God hath wronged me in my cause,
Behold, I cry out "Violence!"
But I am not heard;
I cry for help,
But there is no justice.
He hath put my brethren far from me,
And mine acquaintance are wholly estranged from me.
My kinsfolk have failed,
And my familiar friends have forgotten me.
They that dwell in mine house, and my maids, count me for
    a stranger;
I am an alien in their sight.
My breath is strange to my wife,
Even young children despise me;
Have pity upon me, O ye my friends,
For the hand of God hath touched me!
Why do ye persecute me as God,
And are not satisfied with my flesh?

(*He pauses; peers at* FRIENDS *in appeal: they remain un-
moved. Then with a sudden burst.*)

I know that my avenger liveth,
And that He shall stand up at the last upon the earth!
—My reins are consumed within me—

(*He falls to the ground.* ZOPHAR *tries to help him up,
but* JOB *shrinks away from him.* ZOPHAR *shows he is
offended.*)

If ye say, How we will persecute him!
And that the root of the fault is found in me;
Be ye afraid of the sword:
For wrath bringeth the punishments of the sword,
That ye may know there is a judgment—

ZOPHAR

(*Speaking across* JOB *to* BILDAD.)

I have heard the reproof which putteth me to shame,
And the spirit of my understanding answereth me.

(*Turning to* JOB.)

Knowest thou not this of old time,
Since man was placed upon earth,
That the triumphing of the wicked is short,
And the joy of the godless but for a moment?
He shall not rejoice.
For he hath oppressed and forsaken the poor;
He shall not save aught of that wherein he delighteth.
There was nothing left that he devoured not,
Therefore his prosperity shall not endure.

(*Turning to* BILDAD.)

His goods shall flow away in the day of his wrath.
This is the portion of a wicked man from God.
And the heritage appointed unto him by God.

JOB

Hear diligently my speech,
And let this be your comfort unto me.
(BILDAD *and* ZOPHAR *try to interrupt.*)
Look unto me, and be astonished,
And lay your hand upon your mouth.

For even the memory of this troubles me,
(*His eyes fixed, as if he were seeing a vision.*)
—Wherefore do the wicked live,
Become old, yea, wax mighty in power?
Their houses are safe from fear,
Neither is the rod of God upon them.
Yet they said unto God, "Depart from us,
For we desire not the knowledge of Thy ways.
What is the Almighty that we should serve Him?
And what profit should we have if we pray unto Him?

ELIPHAZ
(*Interrupting.*)

Lo, their prosperity is not in *their* hand:
The defense of the wicked is far from *me*.

JOB

How oft is it that the lamp of the wicked is put out?
How oft cometh their calamity upon them?

BILDAD
(*Interrupting.*)

God layeth up their iniquity for their *children*.

JOB

Let God recompense it unto the wicked himself, that himself may know it!

Let his own eyes see his destruction,
And let *him* drink of the wrath of the Almighty.
For what careth he for his house after him,
When the number of his months is cut off in the midst?

ZOPHAR
(*Interrupting.*)

Shall any teach God knowledge,
Seeing He judgeth those that are high?

JOB
(*With a gesture of despair at his friends' stupidity.*)

One dieth in his full strength,
Being wholly at ease and quiet:
And another dieth in bitterness of soul,
And never tasteth of good.
They lie down alike in the dust,
And the worm covereth them.

(*Interrupting together.*)
ELIPHAZ

God's—

BILDAD

Behold—

ZOPHAR

Wherefore—

JOB
(*Impatiently continuing.*)

Behold, I know your thoughts,
And the devices wherewith ye would wrong me.

For ye say, "Where is the house of the prince?
And where is the tent wherein the wicked dwelt?"
Have ye not asked wayfaring men?
And do ye not know their evidences—
That the evil man is spared in the day of calamity?
He shall be borne to the grave;
And men shall keep watch over his tomb.
The clods of the valley shall be sweet unto him,
And all men draw after him,
As there went innumerable before him.
How then comfort ye me in vain,
Seeing in your answers there remaineth only falsehood.

> (BILDAD, ZOPHAR *leave in disgust through door at
> transept right.* JOB *looks after them a moment, then
> passes to the side of the altar.*
> ELIHU *steps forward by the sacrificial altar at the head
> of the* CHORUS.)

ELIHU
(*Chanting.*)

There are those that remove the landmarks;
They violently take away flocks and feed them.
They drive away the ass of the fatherless—

They take the widow's ox for a pledge,
They turn the needy out of the way.
The poor of the earth all hide themselves.

Behold, as wild asses in the desert the wicked go forth to
their work,
Seeking diligently for their food:
The wilderness yieldeth them bread for their children.

FULL CHORUS

The wicked pass swiftly away upon the face of the waters,
Their portion is cursed in the earth,
Into the ways of the vineyards they turn not;

The worm feeds sweet on them;
They shall be no more remembered.
Yea, even as a tree the unrighteous shall be broken.

A MAN OF THE CHORUS

The murderer who riseth with the light,
He killeth the poor and the needy
And in the night he is a thief.

The eye also of the adulterer waiteth for twilight:
Saying, No eye shall see me,
And he covers his face with a mask.

From out of the populous city men groan
And the soul of the wounded crieth out.
Yet God regardeth not the evil.

FULL CHORUS

Yea, God preserveth these mighty ones by his power,
God giveth them to be in security, and they rest therein,
But His eyes are upon their ways;

They are exalted; yet a little, and they are gone:
Yea, they are brought low, they are taken out of the way as
    all others
And are cut off as the tops of the ears of the grain.
    (JOB *moves to the left side of the transept.* ELIPHAZ *follows, speaking as he goes.*)

ELIPHAZ

Is it any pleasure to the Almighty that thou art righteous?
Or is it gain to Him that thou makest thy ways perfect?
Is it for thy *fear* of Him that He reproveth thee,
That He entereth with thee into judgment?

Is not thy wickedness great?
Thou hast not given water to the weary to drink,
And thou hast withholden bread from the hungry.
Thou, the mighty man, didst own the land,
Didst in honour dwell therein.
But thou hast sent widows away, stripped,
And the arms of the fatherless have been broken.
Therefore snares are round about thee.

Is not God in the height of heaven?
And behold the stars above, how high they are!
Thou sayest therefore, "What doth God know?
Can He judge through the thick darkness?
Wilt thou keep the old way
Which wicked men have trodden?
Who said unto God, "Depart from us;"
And, "What can the Almighty do for us?"

JOB
(*Interrupting.*)

Yet He filled their houses with good things:
While far from me their wicked counsel is.

ELIPHAZ
(*Without heeding the interruption.*)

The righteous see it, and are glad;
And the innocent laugh them to scorn:
(*Going to* JOB.)

Acquaint now thyself with God and be at peace:
Put away unrighteousness far from thy tents,
And lay thou thy treasure in the dust,
Let the Almighty be thy treasure,
And precious silver unto thee.
Then shalt thou delight thyself in the Almighty,
And shalt lift up thy face unto God.
Thou shalt make thy prayer unto Him,
And He will hear thee.

JOB

Oh that I knew where I *might* find Him,
That I *might* come even to His seat!
Yet behold, I go forward,
But He is not there;
And backward,
But I cannot perceive Him:
But He knoweth the way that I take;
When He hath tried me, I shall come forth as gold.
My foot hath held fast to His steps;
His way have I kept, and turned not aside.
But He hath a mind to a thing,
And who can turn Him?
And what His soul desireth,
Even that He doeth.
For He performeth that which is appointed for me:
And many such things are with Him.
Therefore am I terrified at His presence;
When I consider, I *am* afraid of Him.
For *God* hath made my heart faint.
And alone the *Almighty* hath terrified me;
Why is it, that they who know Him see not His ways?

ELIPHAZ

Dominion and fear are with God;
Is there any number to His armies?
And upon whom doth not His light arise?
How then can man be just with God?
Or how can he be clean that is born of woman?
Behold even the moon hath no brightness,
And the stars are not pure in His sight:
How much less man, that is a worm!
And the son of man, which is a worm!
These are but the outskirts of His ways;
And how small a whisper do we hear of Him!
Then the thunder of His power who can understand?

JOB

As God liveth,
My righteousness I hold fast, and will not let it go:
My heart shall not reproach me, so long as I live.

Because I delivered the poor that cried,
The fatherless also, that had none to help him.
The blessing of him that was ready to perish came upon me:
I caused the widow's heart to sing for joy.
I put on righteousness and it clothed me:
My justice was a robe and a diadem.
I was eyes to the blind,
And feet was I to the lame.
I was a father to the needy,
And the cause of him that I knew not I searched out.
And I brake the jaws of the unrighteous,
And plucked the prey out of his teeth.

Then I said, I shall die in my nest,
And I shall multiply my days as the sand.

And now am *I* become *their* song,
Yea, I am a byword unto them.
They abhor me, they stand aloof from me,
And spare not to spit in my face.
For God hath loosed His cord and afflicted me.
Did not I weep for him that was in trouble?
Was not my soul grieved for the needy?
Yet when I looked for good, then evil came:
And when I waited for light, there came darkness.
Therefore is my harp turned to mourning,
And my pipe into the voice of them that weep.

> (*It is now the time for evening prayer. The* CHORUS
> *groups itself about the altar.*)

ELIHU
(*Intoning.*)

Shema Yisrael,
Yahweh elohenu, Yahweh ehad!

SEMICHORUS I

He gives and He takes away!

SEMICHORUS II

Blessed be the name of Yahweh!

FULL CHORUS

Blessed be the name of Yahweh!

> (*Through all this* JOB *alone stands unmoved. The*
> CHORUS *observing this, show their disapproval in vari-*

ous ways. Some spit on him, others pass him with indrawn skirts. Cries of "Sinner in Israel," "Pool of Iniquity" and other cries of derision are heard.)

JOB

(Turning on them suddenly.)

If I walked with falsehood,
And my foot hath hasted in deceit;
Let me be weighed in an even balance,
That God may know mine integrity;

If my land cry out against me,
And the furrows thereof weep together;
If I have eaten the fruits thereof without money,
Or have caused the owners thereof to lose their life:
Let thistles grow instead of wheat,
And cockle instead of barley!

If mine heart have been enticed unto a woman,
And I have laid wait at my neighbor's door:
Or I have withheld the poor from their desire,
Or I have seen any perish for want of clothing,
Or that the needy had no covering,
Then let my shoulder fall from my shoulder blade,
And mine arm be broken from the bone.

If I have made gold my hope,
And have said to the fine gold, Thou art my confidence;

If I have rejoiced at the destruction of him that hated me
Or lifted up myself when evil found him—
Then—

(*He makes a gesture of resignation. Then with sudden force.*)

Oh that I had the indictment which mine adversary hath written!

Surely I would carry it upon my shoulder:

I would bind it unto me as a crown!

Lo, here is my signature—let God reply!

(*He surveys them, turning slowly. For a moment they stand silent. Then* ELIPHAZ *offers to speak.* JOB *turns from him saying:*)

The words of Job are ended!

(ELIPHAZ *looks at* JOB *in despair. Then he leaves through the door at transept left.*)

ELIHU

(*Coming forward slowly from the altar.*)

I am young, and ye are old:

Wherefore I held back, and durst not show you mine opinion.

Behold, I waited for your words,

I listened for your reasons,

Whilst ye searched out what to say.

Yea, I attended unto you,

And, behold, there was none that convinced Job,

Or that answered his words, among you.

(*To* CHORUS.)

They are amazed, they answer no more:

They have not a word to say.

I also will show mine opinion.

I will speak that I may find relief:

I will open my lips and answer.

(*To* JOB.)

Howbeit, Job, I pray thee, hear my speech,
And hearken to all my words.
If thou canst, answer thou me:

I have heard the voice of thy words, saying,
"I am clean, without transgression;
God counteth me for his enemy";
Lo, I will answer thee: in this thou art not just;
For God is greater than man.
Why dost thou strive against Him
Because He giveth not account of any of His matters?
For God speaketh once,
Yea twice, though man regardeth it not.

Twice, yea thrice, with a man;
Doth God work
To bring back his soul from the pit.
Mark well, O Job, hearken unto me:
                    (JOB *offers to speak.*)
Hold thy peace, and I will speak.
                    (*Changing his mind.*)
If thou hast anything to say, answer me:
Speak thou, for I desire to justify thee.
    (ELIHU *waits, looking to* JOB; JOB *turns his back.* ELIHU
    turns to the CHORUS.)
Hear my words, ye wise men,
Far be it from God, that He should do wickedness;
Neither will the Almighty pervert justice.
Is it fit to say to a king, Thou art vile,
Or to nobles, Ye are wicked?
How much less to Him that respecteth not the persons of
    princes,

Nor regardeth the rich more than the poor.

For they all are the work of His hands.

When He hideth His face, who can behold Him?

Whether it be done unto a nation, or unto a man;

It is done that the godless man reign not, that there be none
to ensnare the people.

For when any hath said unto God,

"I have borne chastisement, I will not offend any more.

That which I see not teach Thou me:

If I have done iniquity, I will do it no more,"

(*To* JOB, *who turns his back.*)

Shall His recompense be as thou wilt, that thou refusest it?

Job speaketh without knowledge,

And his words are without wisdom.

(*To the* FRIENDS.)

Would that Job were tried unto the end,

Because of his answering like wicked men.

For he addeth rebellion unto his sin,

And multiplieth his words against God.

(*He pauses for a moment in the attitude of prayer, then
turns to* JOB *again.* JOB *moves away, but* ELIHU *follows
him.*)

Thinkest thou this to be thy right,

Or sayest thou, "My righteousness is more than God's."

That thou askest, What advantage will it be unto thee?

And, "What profit shall I have more than if I had sinned?"

I will answer thee,

And thy companions with thee.

Look unto the heavens and see:

And behold the skies, which are higher than thou.

If thou hast sinned, what effectest thou against God?

And if thy transgressions be multiplied, what doest thou
    unto Him?
If thou be righteous, what givest thou Him,
Or what receiveth He of thine hand?
Thy wickedness may hurt a man as thou art:
And thy righteousness may profit a son of man.
Surely God will not hear an empty cry,
Neither will the Almighty regard it.
How much less when thou sayest thou beholdest Him not:
The cause is before Him, therefore wait for Him!
But now because He hath not visited in His anger,
Thou sayest, He doth greatly regard arrogance:
—Thus doth Job open his mouth in vanity;
He multiplieth words without knowledge.

THE CHORUS

Behold, God is mighty,
And despiseth not any;
He is mighty in strength of understanding.
He preserveth not the life of the wicked:
But giveth to the afflicted their right.
But they that are godless in heart lay up anger:
They cry not for help when He bindeth them.
They die in youth,
And their life perisheth among the unclean.

ELIHU

Yea, God would lure thee out of distress
Into a broad place, where there is no straitness;
But thou art full of the judgment of the wicked:

Take heed, regard not iniquity:
For this hast thou chosen rather than affliction.

(*The organ begins playing with an emphasis on the bass.*)

Behold, God doeth loftily in His power:
Who is a teacher like unto Him?
Who can say, Thou hast wrought unrighteousness?

THE CHORUS

Behold God is great, and we know Him not;
The number of His years is unsearchable.
Yea, can any understand the spreadings of the clouds,
The thunderings of His pavilion?

ELIHU

Behold, He spreadeth His light around Him;
He covereth His hands with the lightning;
And giveth it a charge that it strike the mark.
The noise thereof telleth concerning Him,

(*The music of the organ increases.*)

Yea, at this my heart trembleth,
He thundereth with the voice of His majesty:
And He restraineth not the lightning when His voice is
    heard.
God thundereth marvellously with His voice;
Great things doeth He,
Which we cannot comprehend.

(*The music of the organ rises to a crescendo and then stops suddenly.*)

Hearken unto this, O Job:
Stand still, and consider the wondrous works of God.
Dost thou know the balancings of the clouds,
The wondrous works of Him who is perfect in knowledge?
Canst thou with Him spread out the sky,
Which is strong as a molten mirror?

(*The music begins again.*)

And now men see not the light which is bright in the skies,
But the wind passeth and cleareth them.
Out of the north cometh golden splendor:
God hath upon Him a terrible majesty.
> (*The music grows again to a terrible crescendo.* ELIHU
> *prostrates himself by the altar. The* CHORUS *cowers.*
> JOB *alone stands erect in the center of the chancel steps.*
> *The music melts into a clear, soft but penetrating*
> *voice.*)

THE VOICE
(*Still, small, very penetrating.*)

Who is this that darkeneth counsel by words without
  knowledge?
I will demand of thee, and declare thou unto me.
Where wast thou when I laid the foundations of the earth?
—Declare if thou hast understanding—
Who determined the measures thereof, if thou knowest?
Hast thou commanded the morning since thy days began,
Hast thou entered into the springs of the sea?
Have the gates of death been revealed unto thee?
Hast thou comprehended the earth in its breadth?
Declare if thou knowest it all.

Canst thou lift up thy voice to the clouds,
That abundance of waters may cover thee?
Canst thou send forth lightnings, that they may go,
And say unto thee, Here we are?

Hast thou given the horse his might?
Is it by thy wisdom, that the hawk soareth,
Is it that the eagle mounteth up at thy command,
And maketh her nest on high?

Shall he that cavilleth contend with the Almighty?
He that argueth with God, let him answer it.

> (*The* VOICE *gives way to the roar of the organ which
> fades away in an instant.*)

JOB

I know Thou canst do all things
And that no purpose of Thine can be restrained.

THE VOICE
(*With the same soft, clear penetration.*)

Who then is he that can stand before me?
Who hath first given unto me that I should repay him?
Whatsover is under the whole heaven is mine.

Gird up thy loins now like a man:
I *will* demand of thee, and declare thou unto me.
Wilt thou even annul my judgment?
Wilt thou condemn me, that thou mayest be justified?
Or hast thou an arm like God?
And canst thou thunder with a voice like Him?

Deck thyself now with excellency and dignity;
And array thyself with honor and majesty.
Pour forth the overflowings of thine anger:
And look upon everyone that is proud, and abase him.
Look on everyone that is proud, and bring him low:
And tread down the wicked where they stand.
Then also I will confess of thee
That thine own right hand can save thee.

JOB

Behold, I am of small account; what can I answer Thee?
I lay mine hand upon my mouth.
Once have I spoken—I will not speak again;
Yea twice; I will proceed no further.
I have spoken, but without understanding,
Things too wonderful, which I did not know.
Only by hearsay had I known Thee,
But now mine eye seeth Thee,
And I recant my challenge and am comforted
Amid dust and ashes.

> (*The organ roars up for an instant and then changes
> to soft, peaceful music. The* CHORUS *arises slowly and
> with signs of fear and awe moves out through the
> chancel door.* ELIHU *follows them. In the distance is
> heard the faint intonation of the* CHORUS.)

CHORUS

Hear O Israel,
Yahweh is our God, Yahweh alone,
He gives and he takes away;
Blest be the name of Yahweh forever!

(Throughout this action JOB *stands immovable, his arms pressed over his breast, his head erect. Then he slowly follows the* CHORUS.*)*

NARRATOR

And it was so, that after Yahweh had spoken these words unto Job, the Lord said to Eliphaz the Temanite, "My wrath is kindled against thee, and against thy two friends: for ye have not spoken of me the thing that is right, as my servant Job hath. Now, therefore, take unto you seven bulloks and seven rams, and go to my servant Job, and offer up for yourselves a burnt offering; and my servant Job shall pray for you; for him will I accept; for ye have not spoken of me the thing that is right, as my servant Job hath."

So Eliphaz the Temanite, and Bildad the Shuhite and Zophar the Naamathite went, and did according as Jehovah commanded them: and Yahweh accepted Job.

And so Yahweh blessed the latter end of Job more than his beginning: and he had fourteen thousand sheep, and six thousand camels, and a thousand yoke of oxen, and a thousand she-asses. He had also seven sons and three daughters. And in all the land were no women found so fair as the daughters of Job: and their father gave them inheritance among their brethren.

And after this Job lived an hundred and forty years, and saw his sons, and his son's sons, even four generations. So Job died, being old and full of days.

(The NARRATOR *leaves the pulpit and goes out by the chancel door. The organ plays softly as the congregation leaves.)*

NOTES ON SOURCES AND TRANSLATIONS

THE BIRTH OF JESUS. This play was originally performed by the Tile-Thatchers of York as part of the cycle presented by the guilds of that city in the fourteenth, fifteenth, and sixteenth centuries.

HEROD AND THE KINGS. A twelfth-century manuscript from the Abbey St. Benoit-sur-Loire, France.

THE ANNUNCIATION, THE BIRTH, AND THE SHEPHERDS. This is the first part of the pageant of the Shearmen and Tailors of Coventry, a play which, it is likely, Shakespeare saw as a boy.

THE INNOCENTS. The second part of the pageant of the Shearmen and Tailors.

THE SECOND SHEPHERDS PLAY. This is the second (in date of composition) of two plays about the shepherds in the Wakefield cycle, performed at about the same time as the plays of the York cycle.

ST. NICHOLAS AND THE SCHOLARS, THE FLEURY SEPULCHRE PLAY, and THE JOURNEY TO EMMAUS. All are twelfth-century manuscripts from the Abbey St. Benoit-sur-Loire; the latter two have been newly translated from the Latin, for this volume, by Francis Bliss.

THE KING OF GLORY. This is an early thirteenth-century manuscript from Klosterneuberg, Germany; translated from the Latin and Low German, for this volume, by Francis Bliss.

THE RESURRECTION OF CHRIST. A Wakefield guild cycle play from about the fifteenth century.

THE REDENTIN EASTER PLAY. The manuscript (author conjectural) was completed November 20, 1464 in Redentin, in the principality of Mecklenburg, Germany. The version here printed (much reduced in length) is an adaptation of the translation by A. E. Zucker from the original Low German.

THE RAISING OF LAZARUS by Hilarius. This is the only one of the plays in this volume whose author is known. He was Hilarius, a wandering twelfth-century scholar, presumed to be French. The entire known body of his works is contained in a 32-page volume in the Bibliothèque National, Paris. The translation in this volume is by Francis Bliss.

THE SACRIFICE OF ISAAC. Often called the Brome play of Abraham and Isaac, because the manuscript is preserved at Brome Manor, Suffolk, England, in a commonplace book, dated 1470–1480. This, however, is a transcript of the original play which is presumed to be at least a century older. It is not known whether the play formed part of a cycle, nor is it known where it was originally presented.

THE TRAGEDY OF JOB. This version has been adapted for production in the church from the arrangement by

Horace M. Kallen, published under the title of: *The Book of Job as a Greek Tragedy*. It is Professor Kallen's theory that the Book of Job was originally written in imitation of Greek tragedy, the work of a writer much influenced by Greek culture.

NOTES ON PRODUCTION

Staging in the Church
(*See floor plan, p. 2.*)

THE DIRECTIONS suggested for the plays which may be done in the church proper have been based upon the natural division of the floor plan of a typical church. "Transept right" and "transept left" have been used throughout as they are used by the clergy, that is, facing the congregation. The editors are aware that in a few cases the directions given may not suffice for a particular church. They are meant only to serve as a general guide and to impress upon the director the need for making the fullest use of the acting areas—restricted though each may be—which the architectural form of the church provides. They emphasize the necessity for making the physical movement of each play as continuous and active as possible, within the bounds of church dignity and propriety.

It is important to remember that the effectiveness of these plays does not rely upon elaborate scenery and staging. They are simple, naïve expressions of faith and reverence, and it would detract immeasurably from their success if they were not presented with the utmost simplicity. The merest suggestion of scenery, costumes, and properties will be sufficient, and the congregation will be the more deeply affected if its imagination is called upon to supply the major portion of the atmosphere.

No attempt has been made to give directions for those

plays which are suggested for use in the recreation room. The physical arrangement of stage and audience areas must dictate what should and can be done, and the editors have left this to the discretion of the individual director. He must keep in mind, however, a simple, imaginative use of the space at his command.

For example, the *Second Shepherds Play* introduces the problem of three scenes supposedly some distance apart, a problem customarily solved in the theatre by a physical change of scenery, or by elaborate lighting shifts. Neither of these solutions is essential, nor even superior, to a change in the focus of attention of the audience. It is quite practical to place all three scenes simultaneously upon a very small stage. The field needs no indication not given by the lines and can be the neutral space downstage of center; MAK's house can be indicated left or right by a bed and a crib; the scene in Bethlehem by the manger. If the actors who are not involved in a scene remain motionless at their places, they will in no way distract the audience from the action, for audience attention is directed towards movement and speech. When these principles are observed none of the plays included here will be found too difficult for production with even the most limited of facilities.

Scenery

THE PLAYS for the Christmas season require only one piece of scenery, the cattle shed in Bethlehem (see Typical Church Floor Plan facing page 3). This alone is essential, because of the references within the plays to the "beasts" that "warm the Christ child with their breath." They can only, practicably, be represented as painted upon the scene. This piece of scenery may be quickly and easily constructed as shown on page 257.

The plays for the Easter season, too, require but one piece of scenery, the sepulchre, which may be built as shown on page 259. A tomb of similar construction may be used for *The Raising of Lazarus.*

The Sacrifice of Isaac and *The Tragedy of Job* both call for a "sacrificial altar." This piece of scenery may be easily constructed or improvised by the use of a large packing box or a table, covered with a soft, dark cloth. In the case of *The Sacrifice of Isaac,* firewood can be piled around the bottom of the altar in order to enhance the symbolical illusion.

Apart from the three pieces described above, no other scenery will be found necessary. However, it may be found advisable, where characters are required to kneel, sit, or lie down for any length of time in the transept, to provide a small platform, in order to lift the actors high enough for them to be seen. The important thing to remember about the physical production of these plays is that stylization and suggestive staging will call forth the participation of the congregation's imagination much more effectively than any attempt at realism in scenery and staging.

Properties

OF THE PROPERTIES for plays in this volume, only two pose a problem: the star above the manger in the nativity plays, and the ram in *The Sacrifice of Isaac.* As suggested in the section on scenery, the star may be regarded as a part of the manger setting, since it is attached to the roof of the shed. Individual directors may find it desirable to vary this appearance by building a star of paper or cloth over a wire

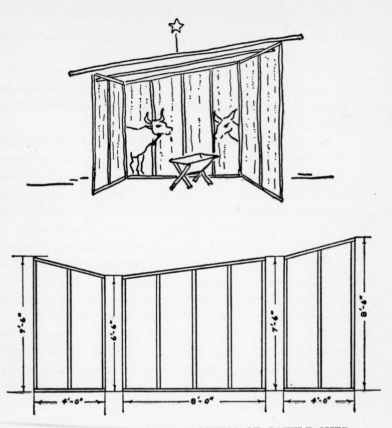

SKETCH AND SCALED DRAWING OF CATTLE SHED

Frames of 2″x2″ lumber, hinged at corners

Two rafters to extend 1′ over each side

Uneven diagonal braces as in sketch, cut from Beaverboard
and tacked on back of screens

Back of screens hung with gray, tan, or other neutral dra-
peries in fullness

Wood of screens stained or painted soft warm gray or tan

Star made of cardboard covered with foil—supported by
wire

Cutouts of ass and ox can be made of Beaverboard and
fastened to screens

framework, illuminating it from within by a light bulb
fastened to the internal framework. This is not essential,
however, as the star is to serve merely as a symbol, and in
the majority of cases a cutout star covered with tin foil will
be found entirely satisfactory.

At first glance, the ram in *The Sacrifice of Isaac* and the
sheep in *The Second Shepherds Play* may seem to be insur-
mountable obstacles, but here, again, is a case where suggestion is more effective than realism. If the director will let the
sheep be carried, he will thus eliminate the necessity for its
being able to stand up. Under those circumstances it is a
simple matter to make a large cardboard cutout in the shape
of a sheep. Using this cutout as a pattern, pieces of cloth
(muslin or cotton) may be cut to the same shape. If two
such pieces of cloth are sewed together, they form an ex-
cellent mold which can then be stuffed until a very con-
vincing representation of a sheep has been created. The
perfectionist property mistress may then put finishing
touches on this form by covering it with cotton and sup-
plying it with a painted face.

All other properties in the plays are of the simplest kind,
and very easily located. They consist of chairs, tables, books,
etc., which may be collected within the precincts of the
church itself.

Lighting

No ELABORATE lighting equipment or arrangement is necessary for production. The general church illumination will
be quite sufficient, augmented from time to time by the use
of candles. Where desired, the star used in the Christmas
plays may be given more dramatic emphasis by additional

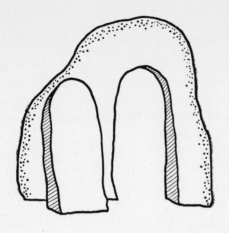

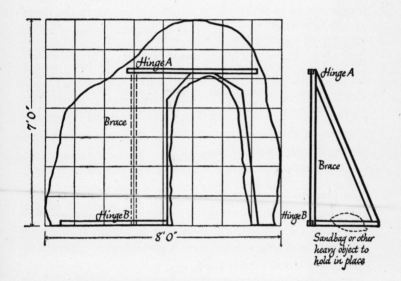

Hinge A

Brace

Hinge B

7'0"

8'0"

Hinge A

Brace

Hinge B

Sandbag or other
heavy object to
hold in place

SKETCH AND SCALED DRAWING OF TOMB

Cutout of Beaverboard, opening reinforced with wood to
which is tacked 8″ strips of Beaverboard thickness

Edges of piece cut from entrance likewise reinforced and
given thickness as in sketch

Painted a soft gray—edges darker to suggest dimension

illumination, but such detail is not required in stylized production of this kind.

Music

IN THEIR ORIGINAL productions, most of these plays were either chanted or played against a musical background. It is suggested that the director make the fullest possible use of music: to bridge from scene to scene with an organ passage, or to underline the action on the organ, or to punctuate and extend the climaxes by means of organ or choir.

The editors have included the musical notation for certain songs which seemed to require original composition or are difficult to locate in church music libraries. They have left to the discretion of the director the selection of hymns and organ music indicated throughout the text, believing that these must be suited to the needs of each congregation.

Costumes

THE DIRECTOR customarily faces with a great deal of trepidation the problem of costuming such period drama as these plays for the church. He feels that historical accuracy is necessary and that this requires a good deal of research in design and detail in execution.

These are unnecessary fears in the preparation of costumes for *stylized* period plays. The audience will willingly cooperate with the director in his attempt to create an illusion, so that it is not necessary to enter into the extravagant lavishness displayed in period motion pictures. In the case of

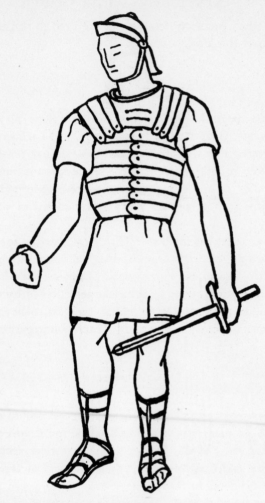

SOLDIER

(Add a cloak for Pilate)

KING

(Use a different crown for Herod)

ANGEL

(Suitable for Jesus and for St. Nicholas. Add wig and beard for God)

MARY

(Suitable for Mary the Mother, the three Marys, the Women, and the Sisters of Lazarus)

PILGRIM

*(Suitable for Joseph and the Scholars. Without staff and
wallet, suitable for the Disciples, the Friends of Lazarus,
the Old Man, the Watchman, and the Messenger)*

PRIEST (CAIAPHAS)

(Suitable for Job and his friends, for Abraham)

SHEPHERD

(Suitable for Isaac)

Fourteen Plays for the Church the designer's sole concern should be to achieve a certain atmosphere of Biblical times, and—with each individual costume—a feeling of type and social status.

For example, the accompanying sketch of a king's costume gives us no particular historical king, nor even an accurate picture of kings in a particular period. But it does aid the congregation, by means of the simplest suggestions, to conjure up the image of "a king." When this approach to the costuming problem is adopted, it will be readily seen that the difficulties of costuming are far more imaginary than real.

In the accompanying sketches, the editors have suggested seven basic designs which can be used as starting points for the costuming of almost every character in the fourteen plays. If the individual designer, taking cognizance of the fact that the sketches portray costumes which are extremely easy to construct, will work from them, adding to or subtracting from them according to his own imagination, he should find it comparatively easy to arrive at some compromise ideally suited to his group.

Although these production notes have stressed simplicity —at times bordering almost on austerity—throughout, and although this suggestion has been repeated here in regard to basic costume design, it is recommended that in the matter of *color* some departure may be made from that pattern. A bold and imaginative use of color in the costumes will not be out of keeping with the dignity of the church, and will, at the same time, help to make the plays exciting, dramatic, and infinitely more appealing to the eye.

THE SONG OF THE KINGS

Wilton Mason

THE SONG OF THE KINGS (cont.)

pro - phets fore - told, it has come — to — pass — He

lies in the straw with the ox and the ass,— But the star — ri - ses

bright, His vi - gil to keep; — It shines — and it

blinds our eyes with its light. —

TERLI TERLOW

Wilton Mason
(simply as in a folk-song)

With smooth, swinging rhythm

As I rode out this poco past mid-night, Of three jol-ly shep-herds I caught a sight, And all a-bout their fold a star shone bright — They sang ter-li ter-low, ter-li — ter-

TERLI TERLOW (cont.)

low, _____ So mer - ri -ly— the shep-herds their pipes can

blow. _____

LULLY LULLAY

Not too slow
Refrain

End here

(verse 3)

After 3rd verse, sing refrain agai

SING IVY

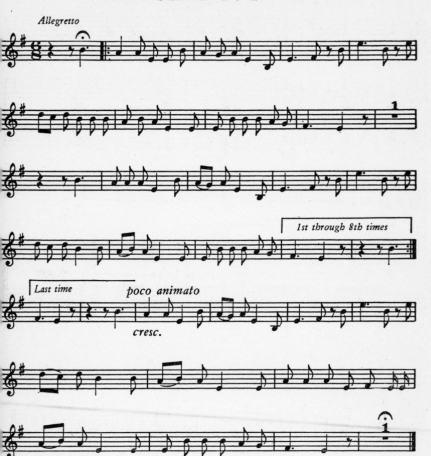

THE KING OF GLORY

Wilton Mason

THOU ART HERE*

Broadly - well sustained

Wilton Mason

1. Thou art here. De - sire of Na - tions;
2. Thee we've called u - pon with sigh - ing,

Long in — dark - ness we have lain! — Lead us out, oh
In our — time of trou - ble, Thee! — Thou the hope of

Lord, this night, From pri - son and — from pain! —
hope - less men, A' rock in mi - se - ry! —

...ay be used as a 4 part mixed chorus by assigning the voice parts to the appropriate stratum in ...accompaniment.